Philosophy of History

Alan Donagan

INDIANA UNIVERSITY

Barbara Donagan

Sources in Philosophy

A MACMILLAN SERIES

Lewis White Beck, General Editor

THE MACMILLAN COMPANY, NEW YORK

COLLIER–MACMILLAN LIMITED, LONDON

901
D67p

First Printing

Library of Congress catalog card number: 65-11879

THE MACMILLAN COMPANY, NEW YORK

COLLIER-MACMILLAN CANADA, LTD., TORONTO, ONTARIO

Printed in the United States of America

To Raymond Maxwell Crawford
and to the memory of
George Andrew Paul

Acknowledgments

We desire to offer our thanks to Professor Lewis White Beck, our general editor, for his prompt and invariably valuable advice and criticism; to Mr. Moltke S. Gram, who helped us in many ways, besides translating the passage we selected from Ranke's *Ueber die Epochen der neueren Geschichte;* and to Dr. R. A. Miller, Indiana University Librarian, for providing us with a study in the library stack, without which our work would have been immeasurably more difficult.

A.D.
B.L.D.

Contents

Introduction

Philosophy of history may be divided into a critical part and a metaphysical or speculative part.

Critical philosophy of history resembles philosophy of science. It is a philosophical inquiry into history considered as the scientific discovery and explanation of past human actions—that is, into "historiography"—and it treats of such topics as the relation of historical inquiry to other forms of inquiry, the nature of historical truth and the possibility of attaining it, and the nature of historical explanation.

Metaphysical or speculative philosophy of history, on the other hand, like the sort of metaphysical inquiry which Leibniz called "theodicy," [1] endeavours to determine the meaning and purpose of history considered as the totality of past human actions. Some speculative philosophers of history discern its meaning and purpose in a goal to be attained at some future time (for example, the classless state, as Marx held), or in a pattern which they profess to detect in it (for example, a continuous progress, whether material or spiritual, as Comte and J. S. Mill held, or a cyclic movement, as Vico held); others maintain that the meaning and purpose of history lie outside time altogether, in an eternity entered by the elect either at a Last Judgment, or in this life at a "point of intersection of the timeless with time." [2] Yet others consider it a delusion that history has any meaning or purpose at all.

CHRISTIAN THEOLOGY AND SPECULATIVE PHILOSOPHY OF HISTORY

The Fathers of the Christian Church preached a speculative interpretation of history which has never failed to captivate adherents. They taught that the purpose of each individual human life is to achieve, by grace, a proper relation to God. From this point of view, history is the record of God's transactions with man, and at

---

[1] "Theodicy" originally meant a vindication of the goodness and justice of God in face of the existence of evil; it is now sometimes used in an extended sense, to mean any attempt to show that, although there is evil in it, the universe is at bottom good. Hegel described "the true *Theodicaea*" as "the justification of God in History."

[2] T. S. Eliot, *The Dry Salvages*, Part V. In *Little Gidding* Part V, Eliot condensed this interpretation of history into a single epigram: "History is a pattern/Of timeless moments."

its center is the life of Christ—his incarnation, passion, and resurrection. Before Christ, history began with the fall of Adam, to which the original sin of all mankind can be traced. From Adam to Christ, history was a preparation for the salvation of man through Christ, the second Adam. This preparation St. Augustine divided into five periods or ages: from Adam to Noah's flood; from the flood to Abraham; from Abraham to David; from David to the captivity in Babylon; and from the captivity to the birth of Christ. We are in the sixth age, which "is now passing," but which "cannot be measured by any number of generations, as it has been said, 'It is not for you to know the times, which the Father hath put in his own power'" (p. 33). A seventh, or millenial age, which St. Augustine described as "our Sabbath" will follow; and it "shall be brought to a close, not by an evening, but by the Lord's day, as an eighth and eternal day . . . This is what shall be in the end without end" (p. 34).

The whole course of history is therefore providential. God, "who by His providence and omnipotence distributes to every one his own portion, is able to make good use not only of the good, but also of the wicked" (p. 26). Yet, like the other Fathers of the Church, St. Augustine did not venture to explain the providence he so forcibly announced. For he never wavered in his conviction that every human action is freely chosen. "All was brought about in such a manner that neither did any future event escape God's foreknowledge, nor did His foreknowledge compel any one to sin . . ." (p. 26).

Except in outline, St. Augustine did not think that the design of divine providence had been revealed to us; he considered it presumptuous to profess to know what God has not revealed. He relished St. Paul's exclamation: "How unsearchable are his judgments, and his ways past finding out" (Rom. 11:33). For the present, since Christians cannot know why the wicked often prosper and the good are often afflicted, "it is salutary for us to learn to hold cheap such things, be they good or evil, as attach indifferently to good men and bad, and to covet those good things which belong only to good men . . ." (p. 32). Our consolation is that, at the Last Judgment, we shall not only "recognize the justice of all God's judgments," but "we shall also recognize with what justice so many, or almost all, the just judgments of God in the present life defy the scrutiny of human sense or insight . . ." (p. 32).

Although he discouraged Christians from superficial interpretations of historical events as divine judgments, St. Augustine did not hesitate to declare that "this whole time or world-age" is the career of what he "mystically" called two "cities." The human race can be divided into those who live according to man (the earthly city), and those who live according to God (the heavenly city, or city of God). Citizens of the heavenly city also belong to the earthly one, in which genuine goods are attainable: law and order, peace and plenty. But if the members of the earthly city "neglect the better things of the heavenly city, . . . and so inordinately covet these present good things that they believe them to be the only desirable things . . . then it is necessary that misery follow and ever increase" (p. 28). Hence, although he did not profess to fathom the operations of divine providence in particular cases, St. Augustine did offer a general explanation for the internal and external strife which has destroyed every earthly society. Unless its citizens owe their first allegiance to the heavenly city, the earthly city is divided against itself.

A philosopher cannot escape the question: Is the traditional Christian philosophy of history, which St. Augustine perfected, true? Is history "universal, providential, apocalyptic, and periodized" (p. 23) in the way in which St. Augustine believed? What were St. Augustine's own reasons for believing it?

Neither St. Augustine nor any other Father of the Church professed to arrive at his philosophy of history by studying history. It was to the Scriptures, not to the writings of historians, that they appealed, and they read the Scriptures as theologians. Believing everything in the Scriptures to be true, because it is from the source of all truth, they regarded scriptural problems as problems of theological interpretation. Nothing fundamental in St. Augustine's *City of God* rests on any belief which he accepted on historiographical evidence. It is true that St. Augustine accepted from the Roman historians the belief that Romulus, the founder of Rome, was a fratricide like Cain; but his philosophy of history is not jeopardized by the discovery that the story of Romulus and Remus is a myth. A discovery that the story of Cain and Abel is mythical would be a different matter; for it would call in question St. Augustine's assumptions about the use of the Scriptures.

Today, many Christians would concede that the Scriptures contain mythical elements, and that their human authors, although divinely inspired in matters of faith, remained men of their time in historiography as well as in natural science. Such Christians require Christian philosophers of history to disentangle the essential Christian interpretation from the out-of-date dress in which the Fathers of the Church presented it. As the selection from Herbert Butterfield shows, St. Augustine's work survives this "demytholigizing" remarkably well. Butterfield only echoes St. Augustine when he observes that "we may feel that we are studying the ways of Providence, but we cannot say that we have demonstrated the existence of Providence," and when he warns believers that "the attempt to vindicate Christianity in history easily turns into an attempt to justify Christians instead." And, although he has abandoned St. Augustine's biblical periodization, he continues to divide history apocalyptically into a part looking forward to the incarnation of Christ, and a part looking backward to it. Nor does he doubt that God was in fact incarnate in Jesus of Nazareth. It is true that some modern theologians are prepared to doubt it. Paul Tillich, for example, has written:

> In 1911 . . . I raised and attempted to answer the question, how the Christian doctrine might be understood, if the non-existence of the historical Jesus should become historically probable. Even today, I maintain the radicalism of this question over against compromises . . . The foundation of Christian belief is not the historical Jesus, but the biblical picture of Christ. The criterion of human thought and action is not the constantly changing and artificial product of historical research, but the picture of Christ as it is rooted in ecclesiastical belief and human experience." [3]

While St. Augustine would have applauded Tillich's denial that the biblical picture of Christ is a product of historical research, he would have denounced Tillich's inference that a Christian is not called upon to affirm that picture of Christ as historically true.

THE FOUNDATIONS OF CRITICAL PHILOSOPHY OF HISTORY: DESCARTES TO VICO

The possibility of conflicts between the Scriptures and the results of historiography is now commonly acknowledged. But it is often overlooked that such conflicts would not matter at all unless his-

[3] *The Interpretation of History*, New York, Scribner's, 1936, pp. 33–4.

toriography could claim scientific status. If St. Augustine had been confronted with a conflict between the Scriptures and a Greek or Roman historian, he would undoubtedly have refused to take the historian seriously. No Greek philosopher had ever considered historiography to be a science: Aristotle's remark that "poetry is a more philosophical and a higher thing than history" [4] was typical. And, as our selection from Descartes shows, the father of modern philosophy was as little inclined as the Greeks to recognize that historians could establish anything with scientific certainty. In philosophy of history Descartes did not try to improve on St. Augustine. "I honoured our Theology," he wrote, "and aspired as much as anyone to reach to heaven, but having learned . . . that the revealed truths that conduct us thither are quite above our intelligence, I should not have dared to submit them to the feebleness of my reasonings." And he would have been horrified had any historian dared to do so, for even in "the most accurate of histories" he considered that "what is retained is not portrayed as it really is" (p. 43).

Given the state of historiography in his day, Descartes's scepticism was amply justified. Yet his criticism, and his theories of method in the natural sciences, provoked and encouraged historians to improve their methods. By the end of the seventeenth century, the century of Descartes, the foundations of the scientific use of many special kinds of historical evidence had been laid: for example, of epigraphy, paleography, diplomatics, numismatics, and sigillography. As Marc Bloch has written, the year of the publication of Mabillon's *De Re Diplomatica*, 1681, "was truly a great one for the history of the human mind, for the criticism of the documents of archives was definitely established." [5] But although the special historical sciences apply methods common to all historiography, those who, like Mabillon, worked out the principles of these sciences, overlooked the need for a general account of historical method comparable to Descartes's and Bacon's accounts of the method of natural science. When Giambattista Vico published such an account in his *Principles of a New Science of the Nature of Nations* (1st ed., 1725, 2d ed., 1730), while admired by some, it was not understood. The importance of the *New Science*

---

[4] *Poetics*, Chap. 9, 1451b 5–7.
[5] Marc Bloch, *The Historian's Craft*, trans. Peter Putnam (Manchester: University of Manchester Press, 1954), p. 81.

(as it came to be called) was not generally recognized in Europe until Michelet translated it into French in 1827.

Against Descartes's teaching that the world of nature, to which the methods of mathematical physics are applicable, is the most fruitful object of scientific study, Vico laid down the principle that man can only fully know what man has made. "Whoever reflects on this," he wrote, "cannot but marvel that the philosophers should have bent all their energies to the study of nature, which, since God made it, He alone knows; and that they should have neglected the study of the world of nations or civil world, which, since men had made it, men could hope to know" (p. 44).

The New Science was to combine two methods: "the philosophical" and the "philological." Each, by itself, Vico considered inadequate. Philosophical method he appears to have conceived as drawing inferences about the human mind in general from one's knowledge of the modifications of his own mind, which are open to his reflection here and now. Philological method, by contrast, is fundamentally the same as that of historiography. A "philologian" tests his hypotheses about what men have thought by inquiring whether what the men in question have "made," especially their languages, literatures, laws, and customs, can be "directly, easily, and naturally," interpreted according to those hypotheses. For example, since the mythologies which men have made can be understood on the hypothesis that those who made them were "naturally poets" recording their "civil histories" in poetic form, Vico considered that hypothesis, and the deductions about the civil histories of the societies which produced those mythologies, to be "philologically" proved.

Vico's most famous use of the philosophical method was in establishing a parallel between the sequence of demands that is natural to man—first necessity, then utility, then comfort, then pleasure, then luxury, and finally mad extravagance—and the sequence of the stages of historical development: "the nature of peoples is first crude, then severe, then benign, then delicate, finally dissolute" (p. 48). It is fascinating to follow him as he shows how "the human necessities or utilities of social life," as they manifest themselves in individuals, and without those individuals intending it in the least, give rise to the same cycle of development in every nation. But although he believed that every nation successively traverses the same sequence, he did not, as R. G. Collingwood has pointed out, conceive the resulting process as "a mere rotation . . . through a cycle of fixed phases"; it is, he thought, "not a circle but a spiral; for history never repeats itself but comes round to each new phase in a form differentiated by what has gone before." [6] Philosophical method, however, treats of what is "perpetually the same" in each cycle.

While the philosophical method, according to Vico, yields truth, the philological is needed for certainty. In the past "the philosophers failed by half in not giving certainty to their reasonings by appeal to the authority of philologians" (p. 50). The glory Vico claimed for his New Science was that it was the first to verify its philosophical results by philological proofs.

By his new combination of methods, Vico professed to have conclusively demonstrated a new speculative philosophy of history. Of course he did not call it that: his name for it was "a rational civil theology of divine providence" (p. 47). For if every society must traverse the stages laid down by his law of development, then he was entitled to infer, as a Christian, that it is by providence that the "universal and eternal" sequence of "forms of order" has been given to "this great city of the human race" (p. 47).

It would be wrong to imagine that Vico intended his theory of providence to supersede the Augustinian one. We have no reason to suspect that he rejected St. Augustine's superrational noncivil theology of what divine providence has in store for the heavenly city, which, as a Catholic, he had been brought up to accept. In Augustinian terminology, he was propounding a rational, that is, a nonrevealed, theory of the providential course of the earthly city. About this, lacking the guidance of revelation, St. Augustine had been piously and prudently silent.

Vico's achievement in critical philosophy of history was of the first magnitude. His principle that what men have made, men can hope to know, is the foundation of modern scientific historiography. First, it defines what historians study: namely, whatever survives from past human actions. Secondly, it implicitly specifies their aim: to recover the human thinking, however different from our own it may have been, by which what survives from the past was made.

Not only did Vico enunciate a host of lesser principles of historical method, for example, the principle that "uniform ideas originating

[6] R. G. Collingwood, *The Idea of History* (Oxford: Clarendon Press, 1946), pp. 67–68.

among entire peoples unknown to each other must have a common ground . . ." (*cf.* p. 45), in his fundamental principle he implied that not only truthful testimony by observant witnesses, but every survival of past human actions, is potential historical evidence. Mythologies and popular traditions which, taken at face value, are absurd, can disclose much to a competent historian about the thinking of the peoples who created them. In his reconsructions of early Roman history, Vico used such evidence ingeniously, and, in many cases, modern research has confirmed his results. His seventeenth-century predecessors had partly anticipated him in practice, by demonstrating that, while a forged document can tell you nothing about its purported author, it can tell you a great deal about its forger.

Yet Vico's critical philosophy of history cannot be pronounced wholly satisfactory. Its fundamental defect is his doctrine that purely "philosophical" proofs of general historical truths are possible. It recalls a defect in Descartes's methodology of physics, which the example of Newton was to expose, but which was not generally perceived in Vico's time. About the discovery of causes in physics Descartes declared that "if the only principles we use are such as we see to be self-evident; if we infer nothing from them except by mathematical deduction; and if these inferences agree accurately with all natural phenomena; then we should . . . be wronging God if we were to suspect [our results] to be delusive." [7] Descartes's use of self-evident principles and mathematical deductions from them corresponds to (although it is not the same as) Vico's "philosophical" proofs; and his use of agreement with all natural phenomena corresponds to (although neither is it the same as) Vico's "philological" proofs.

What is wrong with Vico's philosophical proofs, taken in themselves? Roughly, they divide into two. Proofs like those of the universality of marriage and burial depend on analyses of the concepts involved: they show that all human societies observe those customs because a society that did not would not be "human" but "feral." (Incidentally, "marriage" and "burial" must be understood in very extended senses: for example, "burial" should be taken to include the Parsee practice of exposing the dead on towers to vultures.) By contrast, proofs like that of the sequence of

[7] *Descartes: Philosophical Writings,* trans. G. E. M. Anscombe and P. T. Geach (Edinburgh: Thomas Nelson & Sons Ltd., 1954), pp. 223–224.

human demands depend fundamentally on self-observation. But is it impossible that a man or a society should fail to make the transition from one of Vico's stages to the next, or should miss a stage? And is it certain that only Vico's stages are possible? Vico seems to have misapplied his own principle. It is one thing to say that men can hope to know what men have made; it is quite another to assume that nobody can make anything which you, a philosopher reflecting on your own mind, cannot know in advance. So interpreted, Vico's principle becomes arrogant folly.

Vico's "rational civil theology of divine providence" cannot be proved except philosophically. *Ex hypothesi,* it cannot appeal to revelation; and philological proofs, which Vico conceived to refer to particular societies and times, cannot demonstrate anything universal and eternal. Therefore, if Vico's philosophical proofs are unsound, it follows that his speculative theory of providence is insecure. Its structure is rickety because of a flaw in his critical theory of historiography.

Just as physics could not advance until Descartes's "self-evident principles" were recognized as being brilliant hypotheses, the only proof of which was their agreement or disagreement with natural phenomena, so historiography could not advance until Vico's "philosophical" principles were recognized as being brilliant historical hypotheses, the only proof of which was "philological"— that is, their agreement or disagreement with historical evidence. Once this is perceived, it becomes evident that Vico left unfinished the task of elucidating what agreement or disagreement with historical evidence is, and how it can be used to prove or disprove an hypothesis.

SECULAR THEODICIES AFTER VICO: HEGEL AND MARX

For a hundred years after the *New Science* was published, philosophers who knew little or nothing of Vico excogitated projects for philosophical history, those of Kant [8] and Hegel being the most interesting today. In the speculative part of their work both Kant and Hegel in certain respects excelled Vico, but neither equaled him in the critical part of it; and the critical weakness which vitiated Vico's speculative results was also fatal to theirs.

[8] For Kant's views, see Immanuel Kant, *On History,* ed. Lewis White Beck (Indianapolis: The Liberal Arts Press, 1963).

Hegel's *Philosophy of History,* edited from notes for courses of lectures he delivered in the 1820's, has been the most influential and is the most readable of his works. Hegel was aware, as Vico was not, that it looks self-contradictory to combine philosophy, which "dwells in the region of self-produced ideas" with historiography, which "remains true to its character in proportion as it strictly adheres to its data" (p. 53). Hegel denied, however, that the contradiction is real. On the one hand, he declared that philosophy can demonstrate that the "Idea" or "Reason" is "the *True, the Eternal,* the absolutely *powerful* essence," and that "it reveals itself in the World" (p. 54). On the other, he claimed that his historiography itself shows that his interpretation of history is "not to be regarded as hypothetical, but as a summary view of the whole" (p. 54). On Hegelian principles, that the results of philosophy and historiography should coincide was to have been expected, for "to him who looks upon the world rationally, the world in turn presents a rational aspect."

The rational aspect which history presented to Hegel was providential. Universal history belongs to the realm of Spirit (*Geist*); and Spirit, being self-contained existence, is essentially free. History, therefore, as Spirit in the process of working out the knowledge of itself, is the story of man's working out the knowledge of freedom. This providential development is periodized: first, in the Oriental world, it was recognized that *one* was free, the ruler, but not that man as such is free; secondly, the Greeks and then the Romans, in their different ways, grasped that more than one was free, but not that all are, for "maintenance of their splendid liberty was implicated with the institution of slavery;" finally the Germanic (*germanisch,* not *deutsch*) nations attained the consciousness that man, as man, is free (p. 55). But what is the freedom of which man, as man, has been becoming conscious? It is not each man's freedom to do as he likes (for Hegel, that would be merely "subjective") but "the union of the *subjective* with the *rational* will." Each man must recognize, believe in, and will what is common to the sociopolitical whole to which he belongs. Hence "Law, Morality, Government, and they alone, [are] the positive reality and completion of Freedom" (pp. 60–61).

Since the idea of Spirit, according to Hegel, is "a hidden undeveloped essence," it could not be realized in history without a further element—a motive power. That power Hegel found in "the need, instinct, inclination, and passion of man" (p. 58). Individual men do not, for the most part, pursue the exalted ends which providence is accomplishing. Even "world-historical individuals," like Julius Caesar, "whose own particular aims involve those large issues which are the will of the World-Spirit" (p. 59), are "practical, political men" pursuing "personal aims." They are distinguished from their contemporaries by their "insight into the requirements of the time—*what was ripe for development*," not by their "consciousness of the general Idea they [are] unfolding" (p. 59). In all historical change, Spirit or Reason "remains in the background, untouched and uninjured"; by what may be called "the *cunning of reason*," it "sets the passions to work for itself" (p. 60). And, although the ends are glorious which Spirit accomplishes by its cunning use of individual interests, it takes little care of individuals. Hegel's conviction of the reality of providence did not forbid him to regard history as "the slaughter-bench at which the happiness of peoples, the wisdom of States, and the virtue of individuals have been victimized" (p. 57).

For better or worse, the most distinguished of Hegel's followers, and the most influential of Western philosophers of history since St. Augustine, was Karl Marx. Admiring Hegel's careful studies in the social basis of legal and political relations, and agreeing with Hegel's doctrine that individual interests furnish the ultimate motive power of historical change, Marx found it incredible that history should "end by being resolved into 'self-consciousness' as 'spirit of the spirit'" (p. 68). A brilliant hypothesis, that "the anatomy of [Hegel's] civic society is to be found in political economy" (that is, economics), led him to formulate his famous materialist conception of history: that "the mode of production in material life determines the general character of the social, political and spiritual processes of life" (p. 62).

In all societies except the most primitive, Marx held that up to now the mode of production has involved the division of labor and private property. Labor has accordingly been "alienated" from the worker: its products do not belong to him, and he engages in it, not to satisfy a need, but as a means of satisfying other needs (p. 64). The prevailing mode of production determines the way in which labor is alienated, and that in turn determines the classes of society and the relations between them, that is, the social system. Every social system which depends upon alienated labor is divided into two antagonistic classes: those who alienate their labor, and those who control the labor alienated. Such systems are differentiated from one another by differences in the way in which labor is alienated. Just as slavery, feudal serfdom, and working for wages are different forms of alienation, so master and slave, feudal lord and serf, "bourgeois" employer and "proletarian" wageworker are different forms of class division.

In Western history Marx distinguished ancient, feudal, and modern bourgeois periods, according to the form of class division which prevailed in each period. But he thought that at any given period forms of class division may be found other than the one that prevails. In the ancient world a limited amount of feudalism existed because the mode of production on which feudalism rests existed in a limited way side by side with a different prevailing mode. In the same way, a limited amount of capitalism existed in the feudal world. Changes from one social system to another occur when one mode of production replaces another as the prevailing one. Marx described the process as follows. "At a certain stage of their development, the material forces of production in a society come in conflict with . . . the property relations within which they had been at work before. From forms of development of the forces of production these relations turn into their fetters. Then comes the period of social revolution. With the change of the economic foundation the entire immense superstructure is more or less rapidly transformed" (p. 63).

Historians will always owe Marx a debt for forcing upon their attention the relation between modes of production and social systems, and for proposing a number of original and fruitful hypotheses about it. To Marx himself, however, these achievements were secondary. His philosophy of history is essentially apocalyptic, although the salvation he reveals, unlike that of Christianity, is to be effected in this world. Whereas in all social revolutions hitherto one class has merely displaced another, in the next class system itself will be destroyed. "If the proletariat triumphs this does not mean that it becomes the absolute form of society, for it is only victorious by abolishing itself as well as its opposite. Thus the proletariat disappears along with the opposite which conditions it, private property" (p. 67). This revolution will put an end to "the prehistoric stage of human society" (p. 63).

Neither Hegel nor Marx ventured, like Vico, to set limits to what man could achieve in the earthly city. Hegel refused to predict the future at all. He claimed only to know "the point which consciousness has attained." [9] Marx, it is true, predicted not only a social revolution, but the kind of society that would follow it; yet he did so only because he believed that the material conditions for the overthrow of bourgeois society had almost completed their development within its womb. Believing that the prevailing mode of production determines social relations, he conceived his predictions as no more than statements of the social relations required by a mode of production which already existed, and which was plainly becoming dominant. What man would do when class antagonism was destroyed, when the prehistoric stage of human society was over, he did not venture to say.

HISTORIANS' CRITICISMS OF HEGEL AND MARX

Like Vico, most historians think of historical processes as consisting in the interaction of individual human beings, and as intelligible only in terms of the thoughts and actions of those individuals. Inevitably they are prone to suspect speculative theories such as Hegel's. Thus Leopold von Ranke, perhaps the greatest of the nineteenth century scientific historians, denounced Hegel's doctrine that the World-Spirit "brings things about, as it were, through deceit, and exploits human desires to achieve its ends" (p. 75). If that doctrine were true, it is hard to see how "the largest part of humanity," which "still finds itself in the primitive state," has contrived to escape the attentions of the cunning of reason. To suppose that any part of humanity could do so is at odds with Hegel's declaration that "in the World . . . nothing else is revealed but [the Idea] and its honour and glory." [10] And even in the system of peoples that participate in the general historical movement (roughly, those in western Europe and America), Ranke denied that progress is constant in any fields except those of technology and industry.

Similar objections have been urged by Professor J. N. Findlay, one of Hegel's most sympathetic expositors. "Hegel's own construction," he wrote "pays insufficient regard to the existence of factors which are disruptive and dysteleological . . . It seems a pity that

[9] *The Philosophy of History* (New York: Dover Publications, 1956), p. 456.
[10] *Ibid.*, p. 10.

it recognizes no coexistence of independently significant historical cultures." [11] I cannot understand why Findlay added that "the obvious provincialism of Hegel's philosophical reconstruction of history will not entail that any such reconstruction must be valueless." [12] Hegel himself would have repudiated the suggestion that there could be a plurality of independent self-realizations of the same World-Spirit; and Findlay's admission that "dysteleological" forces may finally prevail is manifestly incompatible with any conceivable theodicy of providence.

The historiographical objections to Marx's speculative philosophy of history are too familiar to require repetition. The social, political, and spiritual (including the intellectual) processes of life are not in the last resort determined by the mode of production in material life: they can and do independently interact with it. Nor are social classes in fact determined by the manner in which labor is alienated. Hence Marx's prediction that the next social revolution would put an end to the alienation of labor, a prediction the fulfilment of which is now in the last degree improbable, would not, even if it were fulfilled, entail the abolition of class antagonism. The end of "the prehistoric stage of human society" has been indefinitely postponed.

Particular historiographical results can be adduced to refute given speculations about the pattern of the historical process; but they cannot preclude the possibility that some as yet unimagined speculative system may turn out to fit them. Even in the present century serious and learned men persist in propounding new speculative interpretations of the course of history for historians to demolish; Spengler and Toynbee are only two of the best known.

Ranke justified his rejection of all such speculative systems on religious as well as on historical grounds. "Every epoch is immediate to God," he wrote, "and its worth does not reside at all in what emanates from it, but rather in its own existence" (p. 74). And again: "I conceive the Godhead—if I may risk this remark— since no time lies in front of it, as surveying all historical humanity in its totality and finding all equally valuable. The notion of the education of the human race has, to be sure, some truth in it. But

[11] J. N. Findlay, *Hegel: A Re-Examination* (New York: The Macmillan Co., 1958), p. 333.
[12] *Ibid.*

before God all generations of humanity have the same rights; and the historian must also see matters in this light" (p. 75).

Ranke's historiographical practice did not conform to his religious convictions; he thought that there was a "general historical movement" in which "only one system of peoples" was taking part (p. 73). Yet it is now a commonplace among historians that Ranke's religious insight was historically better founded than his historiographical practice.[13] While the doctrine that every epoch is immediate to God does not touch the Christian revelation that God has providentially intervened in history, for example at the incarnation, it strikes at the root of all attempts—including Vico's, Hegel's, and Marx's—to show by philosophical and historiographical methods that, without special divine intervention, the course of history has followed an intelligible plan, and that the significance of any epoch lies in its place in that plan. On Ranke's principles, historians may not, as historians, pretend to unravel the secrets of providence, or divide the course of history apocalyptically into a period of darkness and a period of light. Historiography cannot by itself justify theodicy.

HISTORIOGRAPHY AS NATURAL SCIENCE: POSITIVISM AND AFTER

Although by the time of Ranke historiography had become scientific in practice,[14] no adequate critical philosophy of historiography had appeared. Since by then the methodology of the natural sciences was highly developed, it should not surprise us that attempts were made to exhibit historiography as employing the methods of the natural sciences.

Even in the natural sciences two distinct kinds of investigation are possible: into the general laws by which a certain body of

[13] Cf. Gerhard Ritter "Scientific History, Contemporary History, and Political Science," in *History and Theory*, Vol. I (1961), pp. 274–277.

[14] That historiography in the nineteenth century passed through a "scientific revolution," and became a "scientific" study, is generally accepted by its historians: see G. P. Gooch, *History and Historians in the Nineteenth Century* (London and New York, 1913). But when historians like Gooch and philosophers like Collingwood (p. 104) describe modern historiography as scientific, they do not imply that it is a *natural* science like biology. They use "science" in its original sense, as meaning any organized body of knowledge. For various reasons, historiography in the eighteenth century had not become fully scientific (Gooch, *op. cit.*, pp. 10–13; Collingwood, below pp. 98–99).

phenomena may be understood (for example, into the laws of genetics), and into exactly what in the past has given rise to some fact in the present (for example, into the descent of man). Genetics is what Professor Popper has called a theoretical or generalizing science: it is concerned primarily with general laws, and only secondarily with the particular events which fall under them. An investigation into the descent of man, on the other hand, may be thought of as "historical": it is concerned with the particular line of descent from certain primitive forms of life to man as he now is, and only secondarily with the various laws, including those of genetics, by which that descent may be understood.

It is clear that no "historical" investigation in natural science would be possible without a related theoretical or generalizing science. Without his law of natural selection, and a number of hypotheses in what was later to become the science of genetics, Darwin could not have begun his *Origin of Species* or his *Descent of Man*. The only way in which a natural scientist can infer backward from a present event to one past is by supposing that the present event arose out of the past one by some process or processes of which he knows the laws. It is true that if the only evidence Darwin had possessed of the descent of man had been man as he now is, his task would have been impossible: he also needed animal and fossil remains which could be dated on geological grounds. But in its turn the geological past was reconstructed by supposing that the geological present arose out of it by physical and chemical laws which we know.

There is a second respect in which historical natural sciences presuppose generalizing sciences. If a scientist is interested in a particular past event, he will usually try to explain it. The very method by which he traces back a biological line of descent, or the sequence in which the rocks in a given region were deposited, is explanatory; for a given biological or geological state of affairs is explained when you have identified its predecessor and the laws of the processes by which it arose from that predecessor, and have exhibited how it arose according to those laws. Generalizing sciences are needed in explaining past natural events as much as in ascertaining them.

Hence, when a methodologist of natural science is confronted with historiography, the first question you expect him to ask is: On what generalizing sciences does it rest? And until it is answered he will deny that historiographers can possibly possess scientific knowledge that any particular historical event has occurred, much less why it occurred.

John Stuart Mill, in his celebrated *System of Logic,* is a case in point. His chapter on historical method is wholly taken up with how to establish and apply the new generalizing science of sociology, with its two branches of social statics and social dynamics, which had been projected by Auguste Comte. In the first instance, Mill argued, sociologists must obtain their hypotheses empirically, by inductive generalization from the few cases of high social progress which are known. Since such generalizations have weak inductive support, they must constantly be checked by psychological and "ethological" [15] laws. If, granted those laws, we cannot show that our sociological hypotheses are probable or at least possible, we should be very cautious indeed in asserting them.

Mill's proposal that historiography might rest on an empirical sociology, constantly checked by psychology and "ethology," is now a curiosity. Sociology developed in ways other than he had hoped, and "ethology" proved to be chimerical. Nor has Mill's account of the generalizing sciences fully satisfied his more recent successors. Even those who agree with Mill that an "inductive" logic is possible, and that natural science originates with inductively established beliefs, do not dispute that a natural scientist's characteristic procedure is not inductive, but "hypothetico-deductive." Instead of cautiously moving toward a conclusion by accumulating favorable evidence for it, a natural scientist invents hypotheses which are as bold as the facts in his possession will allow; and, taking them together with scientific results considered already established, deduces from them conclusions which can be experimentally checked. An hypothesis is considered established if it satisfies all the experimental tests to which it can in this way be subjected, provided that no bolder and simpler hypothesis will also satisfy them.[16]

---

[15] For the meaning of "ethological," see below, p. 81.

[16] A good elementary account of the hypothetico-deductive method may be found in Morris R. Cohen and Ernest Nagel, *An Introduction to Logic and Scientific Method* (New York: Harcourt, Brace & Co., Inc., 1934), Chap. 11. A more advanced account may be found in K. R. Popper, *The Logic of Scientific Discovery* (New York: Basic Books, 1959), Chaps. 3, 10.

SCIENTIFIC HISTORIOGRAPHY AS INDEPENDENT OF NATURAL SCIENCE: FROM DILTHEY TO COLLINGWOOD

These refinements in the methodology of the generalizing sciences have not succeeded in commending to many historians Mill's doctrine that historiography must rest on some generalizing science. It is true that, when Comte and Mill wrote, few historians ventured to defend their methods. As Wilhelm Dilthey lamented, although their outlook was "deeper and more vital" than that of Comte and Mill, it "had neither firm [methodological] foundations, nor the power to explicate itself" (p. 91).

Yet the historians' position, in Germany especially, was not long without advocates. Not only Dilthey, but Windelband, Rickert, Simmel, and others championed the scientific status of history, and its independence of any generalizing science. Windelband's distinction between the natural sciences as "nomothetic" (that is, generalizing—looking for laws) and the historical sciences as "idiographic" (that is, concerned with describing and comparing individuals) [17] won a considerable vogue. Yet Dilthey's work has worn better than that of his distinguished contemporaries, despite a diffuse and pedantic style which Professor Hodges has described, in a phrase worthy of Dilthey himself, as "a literary veil in some ways uninviting."

Historiography, according to Dilthey, begins with the "manifold forms" in which the human mind has "objectified itself." These objectifications are not only institutions, arts, sciences, and religions, but also physical objects: "every square planted with trees, every room in which chairs are arranged" (p. 93n.). Virtually all our knowledge of what is characteristically human, including our knowledge of ourselves, depends on our power to grasp the incredibly varied mental activities which gave rise to these objectifications. Such knowledge, according to Dilthey, has three foundations: lived experience (*Erlebnis*), expression, and understanding (*Verstehen*). Because our lived experience includes the experience of expressing ourselves, of objectifying our own mental activity, we are able to understand objectifications not only of our own mental activities,

---

[17] W. Windelband, "Geschichte und Naturwissenschaft" in *Praeludien*, Vol. II (5th ed.; Tübingen, 1915). Unfortunately, this essay has not been translated. Windelband's work is discussed by Collingwood, *op. cit.*, pp. 165–168.

but also, by projection, of those of others. Unlike the explanation of a phenomenon in natural science, which requires us to subsume it under some law already known, such understanding is immediate. It requires no knowledge of laws, because it is of the individual state of mind objectified in an individual object. Through understanding, each of us is enabled to relive the lives of others, and his own past life. Without such reliving we could not comprehend the possibilities inherent in human life or even in ourselves. "For me," Dilthey wrote, "as for most people today, the possibility of living through religious experiences in my own person is narrowly circumscribed. But when I run through Luther's letters and writings . . . I live through a religious process of such eruptive power, of such energy, in which the stake is life or death, that it lies beyond any possibility of personal experience for a man of our day" (p. 94).

The end of historiography, according to Dilthey, is the contemplation of past individual mental activities. Such contemplation, he thought, engages an interest "not of the intellect alone, but of the heart, of sympathy, of enthusiasm in which Goethe rightly saw the fairest fruit of historical vision." Hence, he concluded that the sociological theories and the philosophies of history, which see in the description of the singular a mere raw material for their abstractions, are false. While not excluding the possibility of such general theories, Dilthey emphatically denied that they were of the slightest use in historiography.

Discussing Dilthey's work, Collingwood, a recent philosopher who was evidently influenced by it, asked a question that goes to its root.[18] Granted that, through "understanding," you "relive" the past: how can you know that you are doing so? Since Dilthey himself has acknowledged that having a lived experience does not guarantee that you know that you are experiencing it, reliving it cannot guarantee that you know that you are reliving it.

Collingwood's question can only be answered by providing a test for alleged "relivings" of the past. Even in his first book on historiography, his *Introduction to the Human Sciences,*[19] Dilthey recognized that such a test was required, and he suggested that it might be found in a future psychology. Dilthey's projected psy-

---

[18] Collingwood, *op. cit.,* pp. 172–173. In *The Philosophy of Wilhelm Dilthey* (New York: Humanities Press, Inc., 1952), Chap. 10, H. A. Hodges has critically examined Collingwood's criticism of Dilthey.

[19] Published 1883.

chology, however, was as little like the psychology of his own day as it is like that of ours. It was not to be a natural science, as the behaviorist psychology of today is, but a descriptive "typology," or theory of the various human types and their characteristic mental structures; and, like historiography, it was to be constructed by the method of understanding (*Verstehen*).[20] Clearly, this will not do. If it is true that historiographical results arrived at by the method of understanding are in need of verification, then psychological results arrived at by the same impugned method cannot provide it, for they are in need of verification just as much.

Collingwood's answer to his own question, which he implicitly acknowledged to have been anticipated by Benedetto Croce,[21] depended on a sharp distinction between hypothesis in historiography ("reconstruction" was Collingwood's usual term) and verification. Dilthey's method of projection and understanding, as Collingwood saw it, was a true account of how historians make hypotheses about the past, and of the nature of the hypotheses they make. That understanding yields hypotheses, not proofs, has indeed been pointed out by some logical positivists, but they overlooked the crucial point that hypotheses arrived at in this way are individual, not general. Instead of invoking a further science to verify the hypotheses of historians, Collingwood protested that historians themselves had for a century been verifying their hypotheses by the same hypothetico-deductive method as that employed by natural scientists, a method which, rather misleadingly, he described as "Baconian." According to Collingwood, the distinction between the human and the natural sciences is not in their methods of verification, but in the kinds of hypotheses they set out to verify. Those of natural science contain or presuppose putative general laws; those of the human sciences contain or presuppose reconstructions of individual states of mind, but dispense with general laws altogether. Many methodologists seem to have taken it for granted that, unless an hypothesis contains an alleged general law, it is impossible to deduce from it consequences that can be verified or falsified by observable evidence. Collingwood's examples in his *Autobiography* should dispose of that delusion once for all.

[20] H. A. Hodges, *Wilhelm Dilthey: An Introduction* (New York: Humanities Press, Inc., 1944), Chap. 3.
[21] Collingwood, *op. cit.*, pp. 203–204.

THE PRESENT SITUATION

Despite Collingwood's vindication of the established methods of scientific history, Comte's and Mill's ideal of an historiography based on a generalizing science or sciences of man is by no means dead. In our own time, it is persuasively defended by Professors K. R. Popper and C. G. Hempel, both of whom repudiate Mill's doctrine that sociology rests on psychology and ethology. Hempel has modified Mill's position even more radically. Whereas Mill thought of all generalizing sciences as "deductive-nomological," Hempel maintains that "inductive-probabilistic" sciences are also generalizing. If this be accepted, then a demonstration that historiography does not rest on deductive-nomological sciences will not refute Comte's and Mill's position that it rests on generalizing sciences. Hempel goes yet further. Historical explanations, he concedes, are strictly not even inductive-probabilistic; rather, they are sketches of genuine explanations to be achieved in the future. It is hard to refute dreams of future glory.

Hempel's revival and reinterpretation of the positivist ideal has not lacked adversaries, of whom the most learned and articulate is Professor W. H. Dray. While confessing his profound debt to Collingwood, Dray is as little content with Collingwood as Hempel with Mill. He substantially accepts Collingwood's doctrine that historians are concerned with the reasons why historical agents did as they did, but he is uneasy with Collingwood's contention that historiography is Baconian. History, he urges, is one of the humanities; and he is inclined to liken historians more to critics than to scientists.

Can any speculative philosophy of history be derived from critical philosophy of history of the kind embraced by Dilthey and Collingwood? By declaring scientific history to be independent of any generalizing science, they repudiated the necessitation of individual human action by any conditions, internal or external. What an individual can do on a given occasion, even a "world-historical individual," is indeed circumscribed, but it is not predetermined. And, since everything in history arises from the interaction of human individuals, few of whom foresee what others will do in response to what they do, much less the whole pattern of their interaction, neither is the source of history predetermined. Both progress and retrogression are possible. Should history have any "meaning," it would be this: nothing happens in history except as the outcome, usually unforeseen, of free choices by individual men. If history is the slaughter-bench at which the human race is victimized, it is because of what some or all men have done, and not because of ineluctable material necessity or the cunning of the World Spirit.

Is the conception of history as providential then excluded? No. God may intervene in history; but if he has done so, it can be demonstrated neither by historiography nor by philosophy. I think St. Augustine knew that.

R. G. COLLINGWOOD

The Characteristics of Christian Historiography

Robin George Collingwood (1889–1943), lived most of his life in Oxford, where he became Professor of Philosophy. In his autobiography he described his early introduction to archaeology, and the effect of his historical work on Roman Britain on his philosophical development. He had learned from Croce, he once said, "to regard philosophy as primarily the methodology of history." Of his books, An Autobiography *(1939) and* The Idea of History *(1946) are most relevant to his philosophy of history.*

CHARACTERISTICS OF CHRISTIAN HISTORIOGRAPHY

Any history written on Christian principles will be of necessity universal, providential, apocalyptic, and periodized.

(i) It will be a *universal* history, or history of the world, going back to the origin of man. It will describe how the various races of men came into existence and peopled the various habitable parts of the earth. It will describe the rise and fall of civilizations and powers. Greco-Roman oecumenical history is not universal in this sense, because it has a particularistic centre of gravity. Greece or Rome is the centre round which it revolves. Christian universal history has undergone a Copernican revolution, whereby the very idea of such a centre of gravity is destroyed.

(ii) It will ascribe events not to the wisdom of their human agents but to the workings of *Providence* preordaining their course. The theocratic history of the Near East is not providential in this sense, because it is not universal but particularistic. The theocratic historian is interested in the doings of a particular society, and the God who presides over these doings is a God for whom that particular society is a chosen people. Providential history, on the other hand, treats history indeed as a play written by God, but a play wherein no character is the author's favourite character.

(iii) It will set itself to detect an intelligible pattern in this gen-

From R. G. Collingwood, The Idea of History (Oxford: Clarendon Press, 1946), pp. 49–52. Used by permission of the Clarendon Press, Oxford.

eral course of events, and in particular it will attach a central importance in this pattern to the historical life of Christ, which is clearly one of the chief preordained features of the pattern. It will make its narrative crystallize itself round that event, and treat earlier events as leading up to it or preparing for it, and subsequent events as developing its consequences. It will therefore divide history at the birth of Christ into two parts, each having a peculiar and unique character of its own: the first, a forward-looking character, consisting in blind preparation for an event not yet revealed; the second a backward-looking character depending on the fact that the revelation has now been made. A history thus divided into two periods, a period of darkness and a period of light, I shall call *apocalyptic* history.

(iv) Having divided the past into two, it will then naturally tend to subdivide it again: and thus to distinguish other events, not so important as the birth of Christ but important in their way, which make everything after them different in quality from what went before. Thus history is divided into epochs or *periods*, each with peculiar characteristics of its own, and each marked off from the one before it by an event which in the technical language of this kind of historiography is called epoch-making.

All these four elements were in fact consciously imported into historical thought by the early Christians. We may take Eusebius of Caesarea, in the third and early fourth century, as an example. In his *Chronicle* he set himself to compose a universal history where all events were brought within a single chronological framework instead of having events in Greece dated by Olympiads, events in Rome dated by consuls, and so on. This was compilation; but it was a very different thing from the compilations of pagan scholars under the late Empire, because it was inspired by a new purpose, the purpose of showing that the events thus chronicled formed a pattern with the birth of Christ in its centre. It was with this end in view that Eusebius composed another work, the so-called *Praeparatio Evangelica,* in which he showed that the history of the pre-Christian world could be regarded as a process designed to culminate in the Incarnation. Jewish religion, Greek philosophy, Roman law, combined to build up a matrix in which it was possible for the Christian revelation to take root and grow to maturity; if Christ had been born into the world at any other time, the world would not have been able to receive Him.

Eusebius was only one of a large number of men who were struggling to work out in detail the consequences of the Christian conception of man; and when we find many of the Fathers like Jerome, Ambrose, and even Augustine speaking of pagan learning and literature with contempt and hostility it is necessary to remind ourselves that this contempt arises not from lack of education or a barbarous indifference towards knowledge as such, but from the vigour with which these men were pursuing a new ideal of knowledge, working in the teeth of opposition for a reorientation of the entire structure of human thought. In the case of history, the only thing with which we are here concerned, the reorientation not only succeeded at the time, but left its heritage as a permanent enrichment of historical thought.

The conception of history as in principle the history of the world, where struggles like that between Greece and Persia or between Rome and Carthage are looked at impartially with an eye not to the success of one combatant but to the upshot of the struggle from the standpoint of posterity, became a commonplace. The symbol of this universalism is the adoption of a single chronological framework for all historical events. The single universal chronology, invented by Isidore of Seville in the seventh century and popularized by the Venerable Bede in the eighth, dating everything forward and backward from the birth of Christ, still shows where the idea came from.

The providential idea became a commonplace. We are taught in our school text-books, for example, that in the eighteenth century the English conquered an empire in a fit of absence of mind: that is, they carried out what to us looking back on it appears as a plan, though no such plan was present in their minds at the time.

The apocalyptic idea became a commonplace, although historians have placed their apocalyptic moment at all sorts of times: the Renaissance, the invention of printing, the scientific movement of the seventeenth century, the Enlightenment of the eighteenth, the French Revolution, the Liberal movement of the nineteenth century, or even, as with Marxist historians, in the future.

And the idea of epoch-making events has become a commonplace, and with it the division of history into periods each with its own peculiar character.

All these elements, so familiar in modern historical thought, are totally absent from Greco-Roman historiography and were consciously and laboriously worked out by the early Christians.

Christianity and Human Destiny

Born and educated in Roman North Africa, St. Augustine (354–430) did not visit Italy until 383. There he became a Christian; the complex religious, psychological and intellectual influences leading to his conversion are described in his Confessions. *He returned to Africa, and, at forty, became bishop of Hippo, a small seaport which for the rest of his life remained one of the intellectual centers of Christendom. Augustine began* De Civitate Dei *(written between 413 and 426) three years after the sack of Rome by Alaric, an event which, for many Christians, made it difficult to justify the ways of God to man.*

[WHATEVER HAPPENS ACCORDS WITH GOD'S PROVIDENCE]

The sins of men and angels do nothing to impede the great works of the Lord which accomplish His will. For He who by His providence and omnipotence distributes to every one his own portion, is able to make good use not only of the good, but also of the wicked. And thus making a good use of the wicked angel, who, in punishment of his first wicked volition, was doomed to an obduracy that prevents him now from willing any good, why should not God have permitted him to tempt the first man, who had been created upright, that is to say, with a good will? For he had been so constituted, that if he looked to God for help, man's goodness should defeat the angel's wickedness; but if by proud self-pleasing he abandoned God, his Creator and Sustainer, he should be conquered. . . . It was not, indeed, that He was unaware that he should be conquered, but because He foresaw that by the man's seed, aided by divine grace, this same devil himself should be conquered, to the greater glory of the saints. All was brought about in such a manner, that neither did any future event escape God's foreknowledge, nor did His foreknowledge compel any one to sin, and so as to demonstrate in the experience of the intelligent creation,

From *The City of God*, in Vol. II of *Basic Writings of Saint Augustine*, ed. W. J. Oates, pp. 273–276, 455–463, 493–494, 509–517, 660–663, *passim*. Copyright 1948 by Random House. Reprinted by permission of Random House, and of T. & T. Clark, Edinburgh.

human and angelic, how great a difference there is between the private presumption of the creature and the Creator's protection. (xiv, 27)

[THE TWO CITIES: THE EARTHLY
AND THE HEAVENLY]
Accordingly, two cities have been formed by two loves: the earthly by the love of self, even to the contempt of God; the heavenly by the love of God, even to the contempt of self. The former, in a word, glories in itself, the latter in the Lord. For the one seeks glory from men; but the greatest glory of the other is God, the witness of conscience. The one lifts up its head in its own glory; the other says to its God, "Thou art my glory, and the lifter up of mine head." In the one, the princes and the nations it subdues are ruled by the love of ruling; in the other, the princes and the subjects serve one another in love, the latter obeying, while the former take thought for all. The one delights in its own strength, represented in the persons of its rulers; the other says to its God, "I will love Thee, O Lord, my strength." And therefore the wise men of the one city, living according to man, have sought for profit to their own bodies or souls, or both, and those who have known God "glorified Him not as God, neither were thankful, but became vain in their imaginations." . . . For they were either leaders or followers of the people in adoring images, "and worshipped and served the creature more than the Creator, who is blessed for ever." But in the other city there is no human wisdom, but only godliness, which offers due worship to the true God, and looks for its reward in the society of the saints, of holy angels as well as holy men, that God may be all in all. (xiv, 28)

[THIS WORLD-AGE AS THE CAREER
OF THE TWO CITIES]
The human race . . . we have distributed into two parts, the one consisting of those who live according to man, the other of those who live according to God. And these we also mystically call the two cities, or the two communities of men, of which the one is predestined to reign eternally with God, and the other to suffer eternal punishment with the devil. This, however, is their end, and of it we are to speak afterwards. At present, . . . it seems suitable to attempt an account of their career, from the time when our two first

parents began to propagate the race until all human generation shall cease. For this whole time or world-age, in which the dying give place and those who are born succeed, is the career of these two cities concerning which we treat . . . When these two cities began to run their course by a series of deaths and births, the citizen of this world was the first-born, and after him the stranger in this world, the citizen of the city of God, predestinated by grace, elected by grace, by grace a stranger below, and by grace a citizen above. By grace—for so far as regards himself he is sprung from the same mass, all of which is condemned in its origin: but God, like a potter (for this comparison is introduced by the apostle judiciously, and not without thought) of the same lump made one vessel to honor, another to dishonor . . . Accordingly, it is recorded of Cain that he built a city, but Abel, being a sojourner, built none. For the city of the saints is above, although here below it begets citizens, in whom it sojourns till the time of its reign arrives, when it shall gather together all in the day of the resurrection. (xv, 1) . . .

[EXPLANATION OF STRIFE IN THE EARTHLY CITY]

The earthly city . . . has its good in this world, and rejoices in it with such joy as such things can afford. But as this is not a good which can discharge its devotees of all distresses, this city is often divided against itself by litigations, wars, quarrels, and such victories as are either life-destroying or short-lived . . . The things which this city desires cannot justly be said to be evil, for it is itself, in its own kind, better than all other human good. For it desires earthly peace for the sake of enjoying earthly goods, and it makes war in order to attain to this peace . . . Now, when victory remains with the party which had the juster cause, who hesitates to congratulate the victor, and style it a desirable peace? These things, then, are good things, and without doubt the gifts of God. But if they neglect the better things of the heavenly city, which are secured by eternal victory and peace never-ending, and so inordinately covet these present good things that they believe them to be the only desirable things, or love them better than those things which are believed to be better—if this be so, then it is necessary that misery follow and ever increase. (xv, 4) . . .

[GOD'S INTERVENTION IN HISTORY: THE INCARNATION]

While . . . Caesar Augustus was emperor at Rome, the state of the republic being already changed, and the world being set at peace by him, Christ was born in Bethlehem of Judah, man manifest out of a human virgin, God hidden out of God the Father. For so had the prophet foretold: "Behold, a virgin shall conceive in the womb, and bring forth a Son, and they shall call His name Immanuel, which, being interpreted, is, God with us." He did many miracles that He might commend God in Himself, some of which, even as many as seemed sufficient to proclaim Him, are contained in the evangelic Scripture. The first of these is, that He was so wonderfully born, and the last, that with His body raised up again from the dead He ascended into heaven. (xviii, 46) . . .

[THE PROVIDENTIAL GROWTH OF THE CHURCH]

Then was fulfilled . . . the prediction of the Lord Christ himself . . . "that repentance and remission of sins should be preached in His name among all nations, beginning at Jerusalem . . ." First of all, the Church spread herself abroad from Jerusalem; and when very many in Judea and Samaria had believed, she also went into other nations by those who announced the gospel, whom, as lights, He Himself had both prepared by His word and kindled by His Holy Spirit . . . And that they might not be frozen with fear, they burned with the fire of charity. Finally, the gospel of Christ was preached in the whole world, not only by those who had seen and heard Him both before His passion and after His resurrection, but also after their death by their successors, amid the horrible persecutions, diverse torments and deaths of the martyrs, God also bearing them witness, both with signs and wonders, and divers miracles and gifts of the Holy Ghost, that . . . the very kings by whose laws the Church had been laid waste . . . might begin to persecute the false gods for whose sake the worshippers of the true God had formerly been persecuted. (xviii, 50) . . .

[THE NUMBER OF PERSECUTIONS NOT KNOWN BY REVELATION]

I do not think, indeed, that what some have thought or may think is rashly said or believed, that until the time of Antichrist the Church of Christ is not to suffer any persecutions besides those she has already suffered—that is, *ten*—and that the eleventh and last shall be inflicted by Antichrist. They reckon as the first that made by Nero, the second by Domitian, the third by Trajan, the fourth by Antoninus, the fifth by Severus, the sixth by Maximin, the seventh by Decius, the eighth by Valerian, the ninth by Aurelian, the tenth by Diocletian and Maximian. For as there were ten plagues in Egypt before the people of God could begin to go out, they think this is to be referred to as showing that the last persecution by Antichrist must be like the eleventh plague . . . Yet I do not think persecutions were prophetically signified by what was done in Egypt, however nicely and ingeniously those who think so may seem to have compared the two in detail, not by the prophetic Spirit, but by the conjecture of the human mind, which sometimes hits the truth, and sometimes is deceived. But what can those who think this say of the persecution in which the Lord Himself was crucified? In which number will they put it? And if they think the reckoning is to be made exclusive of this one, as if those must be counted which pertain to the body, and not that in which the Head Himself was set upon and slain, what can they make of that one which, after Christ ascended into heaven, took place in Jerusalem, when the blessed Stephen was stoned . . . Why, then, do they think fit to start with Nero, when the Church in her growth had reached the times of Nero amid the most cruel persecutions, about which it would be too long to say anything? . . . When I think of these and the like things, it does not seem to me that the number of persecutions with which the Church is to be tried can be definitely stated. But, on the other hand, it is no less rash to affirm that there will be some persecutions by kings besides that last one, about which no Christian is in doubt. Therefore we leave this undecided, supporting or refuting neither side of this question, but only restraining men from the audacious presumption of affirming either of them. (xviii, 52) . . .

[EXPLANATION OF PEACE AND OF STRIFE BETWEEN THE TWO CITIES]

The families which do not live by faith seek their peace in the earthly advantages of this life; while the families which live by faith look for those eternal blessings which are promised, and use as pilgrims such advantages of time and of earth as do not fascinate and divert them from God . . . Thus the things necessary for this mortal life are used by both kinds of men and families alike, but each has its own peculiar and widely different aim in using them. The earthly city, which does not live by faith, seeks an earthly peace, and the end it proposes, in the well-ordered concord of civic obedience and rule, is the combination of men's wills to attain the things which are helpful to this life. The heavenly city, or rather the part of it which sojourns on earth and lives by faith, makes use of this peace only because it must, until this mortal condition which necessitates it shall pass away. Consequently, so long as it lives like a captive and a stranger in the earthly city, . . . it makes no scruple to obey the laws of the earthly city, whereby the things necessary for the maintenance of this mortal life are administered; and thus, as this life is common to both cities, so there is a harmony between them in regard to what belongs to it. But, as the earthly city has had some philosophers . . . who, being deceived either by their own conjectures or by demons, supposed that many gods must be invited to take an interest in human affairs, and assigned to each a separate function and a separate department: . . . and as the celestial city, on the other hand, knew that one God only was to be worshipped, and that to Him alone was due that service which the Greeks call λατρεία, and which can be given only to a god, it has come to pass that the two cities could not have common laws of religion, and that the heavenly city has been compelled in this matter to dissent, and to become obnoxious to those who think differently, and to stand the brunt of their anger and hatred and persecutions . . . This heavenly city . . . while it sojourns on earth, calls citizens out of all nations, and gathers together a society of pilgrims of all languages, not scrupling about diversities in the manners, laws, and institutions whereby earthly peace is secured and maintained . . . It therefore is so far from rescinding and abolishing these diversities, that it even preserves and adopts them, so long only as no hindrance to the worship of the one supreme and true God is thus introduced. Even the heavenly city, therefore, while in its state of pilgrimage, avails itself of the peace of earth, . . . and makes this earthly peace bear upon the peace of heaven; for this alone can be truly called and esteemed the peace of the reasonable creatures, consisting as it does in the perfectly ordered and harmonious enjoyment of God and of one another in God. When we shall have reached that peace, this mortal life shall give place to one that is eternal, and our body shall be no more this animal body which by its corruption weighs down the soul, but a spiritual body feeling no want, and in all its members subjected to the will. (xix, 17) . . .

[THE INSCRUTABILITY OF GOD'S PROVIDENCE WHEN NOT REVEALED]

In this present time we learn to bear with equanimity the ills to which even good men are subject, and to hold cheap the blessings which even the wicked enjoy. And consequently, even in those conditions of life in which the justice of God is not apparent, His teaching is salutary. For we do not know by what judgment of God this good man is poor and that bad man rich; why he who, in our opinion, ought to suffer acutely for his abandoned life enjoys himself, while sorrow pursues him whose praiseworthy life leads us to suppose he should be happy . . . Who can collect or enumerate all the contrasts of this kind? But if this anomalous state of things were uniform in this life . . . so uniform that none but wicked men won the transitory prosperity of earth, while only the good suffered its ills— this could be referred to the just and even benign judgment of God . . . But now, as it is, since we not only see good men involved in the ills of life, and bad men enjoying the good of it, which seems unjust, but also that evil often overtakes evil men, and good surprises the good, the rather on this account are God's judgments unsearchable, and His ways past finding out. Although, therefore, we do not know by what judgment these things are done or permitted to be done by God . . . , yet it is salutary for us to learn to hold cheap such things, be they good or evil, as attach indifferently to good men and bad, and to covet those good things which belong only to good men . . . But when we shall have come to that judgment, the date of which is called peculiarly the day of judgment, and sometimes the day of the Lord, we shall then recognize the justice of all God's judgments . . . And in that day we shall also recognize with what justice so many, or almost all, the just judgments of God in the present life defy the scrutiny of human sense or insight, though in this matter it is not concealed from pious minds that what is concealed is just. (xx, 2) . . .

[THE TWO RESURRECTIONS AND THE LAST JUDGMENT]

As, then, there are two regenerations . . . —the one according to faith, and which takes place in the present life by means of baptism; the other according to the flesh, and which shall be accomplished in its incorruption and immortality by means of the great and final judgment—so are there also two resurrections—the one the first and spiritual resurrection, which has place in this life, and preserves us from coming into the second death; the other the second, which does not occur now, but in the end of the world, and which is of the body, not of the soul, and which by the last judgment shall dismiss some into the second death, others into that life which has no death. (xx, 6) . . .

[THE HAPPINESS IN STORE FOR THE HEAVENLY CITY]

How great shall be that felicity, which shall be tainted with no evil, which shall lack no good, and which shall afford leisure for the praises of God, who shall be all in all! . . . All the members and organs of the incorruptible body, which now we see to be suited to various necessary uses, shall contribute to the praises of God; for in that life necessity shall have no place, but full, certain, secure, everlasting felicity . . . What power of movement such bodies shall possess, I have not the audacity rashly to define, as I have not the ability to conceive . . . One thing is certain, the body shall forthwith be wherever the spirit wills, and the spirit shall will nothing which is unbecoming either to the spirit or to the body . . . This Sabbath shall appear still more clearly if we count the ages as days, in accordance with the periods of time defined in. Scripture, for that period will be found to be the seventh. The first age, as the first day, extends from Adam to the deluge; the second from the deluge to Abraham, equalling the first, not in length of time, but in the number of generations, there being ten in each. From Abraham to the advent of Christ there are, as the evangelist Matthew calculates, three periods, in each of which are fourteen generations—one period from Abraham to David, a second from David to the captivity, a third from the captivity to the birth of Christ in the flesh. There are thus five ages in all. The sixth is now passing, and cannot be measured by any number of generations, as it has been said, "It is not for you to know the times, which the Father hath put in His own power." After this period God shall rest as on the seventh day, when He shall give us (who shall be the seventh day) rest in Himself. But there is not now space to treat of these ages; suffice it to say that the seventh shall be our Sabbath, which shall be brought to a close, not by an evening, but by the Lord's day, as an eighth and eternal day, consecrated by the resurrection of Christ, and prefiguring the eternal repose not only of the spirit, but also of the body. There we shall rest and see, see and love, love and praise. This is what shall be in the end without end. For what other end do we propose to ourselves than to attain to the kingdom of which there is no end?

I think I have now, by God's help, discharged my obligation in writing this large work. Let those who think I have said too little, or those who think I have said too much, forgive me; and let those who think I have said just enough give thanks, not to me, but rather join me in giving thanks to God. Amen. (xxii, 30)

HERBERT BUTTERFIELD

Christianity and Historical Study Today

Herbert Butterfield (1900–   ), a Cambridge historian, has written extensively on historiography. Among *his best-known books are* The Whig Interpretation of History *(1931)*, Christianity and History *(1954), and* Man on His Past *(1955).*

Over a considerable part of its area history may be conceived to be a science in the sense that it studies very concrete and tangible things, such as can be tested and attested by a definite kind of evidence. Furthermore, it examines the observable or demonstrable connections between those things—the relationships between various kinds of what we call historical "events", for example. Technical history, on this definition, is to be regarded as a mundane and a matter-of-fact affair, and serves only limited purposes. It may provide us with a demonstration that Jesus Christ did live or that a certain saint died at the age of fifty; and if it does prove those points it proves them for all men, whatever their faith—its argument is valid for Catholic or atheist, for Marxist or Mohammedan. There are many things, however—and those much the most important—which the technical historian knows that his evidence and his apparatus give him no special right to decide. Amongst them we should include the quality of Beethoven's music, the rightness of the Reformation and the question of the divinity of Christ. When the technical historian explains the victory of Christianity in the ancient Roman Empire, we should not expect him to say that the success was due to a decree of Providence or to the authenticity of the religion itself. We should rather expect him to provide an empirical study of certain tangible things that gave Christianity its efficacy in the world of that time. There would be many cases where the historian would be aware that he had not found the clinching argument, or fully established even so concrete a thing as a date, or demonstrated his hypothesis to the satisfaction of all his fellow-students. This kind of history, therefore, ought not to appear as a self-complete intellectual system or as a continuous piece of explanation without any holes in it. In reality it is merely the extension of the universal habit of men to reflect on the observable connections between events—beginning, one might say, with the daily rising of the sun, or the experience of the trouble that is likely to be provoked if one steals one's neighbour's food.

If it is asked how this initial view of history—this view of it as a science—is connected with Christianity, or it is argued that so mundane a conception of the subject is actually inconsistent with religion, one may reply that on the contrary there are reasons for suggesting that this approach to any science is a specifically Christian one. It is the view which comes from regarding the historian as a person under a certain kind of discipline for the purpose of examining the ways of Providence and the structure of the providential order. It does not deny Providence. It does not hold that events will form a self-explanatory system without any necessity for the idea of God. It relegates scientific history to a humble rôle, therefore—certainly not assuming that the study of demonstrable events will suffice either to answer the question whether the hand of God can be found in history, or to explain why man exists, or to settle ultimate philosophical problems. And certainly it does not assume, as the Marxists and so many other secularist thinkers seem to do, that when we have learned the history of a thing we shall have achieved its final and total explanation.

The scientific method that we are discussing seems on the whole to have come into existence in the way that has been described—both the natural scientists and the historians acting in the belief that they had found a better means for studying the ways of Providence. And this affected the situation in a definite manner, for it meant that they felt themselves to be operating only on the outer fringe of something far bigger than their instruments and observations could reach. They felt a greater distance between the kind of thinking which analyses a blade of grass more and more minutely or observes the stars over wider and wider expanses of space, and the kind of thinking which estimates the nature of the universe or judges the meaning of life or decides the question of the existence of God. It was discovered that by restricting oneself to the realm of secondary causes, one could pursue certain kinds of more mundane enquiry to better purpose. This is at any rate one of the secrets of the transition to the scientific method of modern times. . . .

It is possible to hold that scientific explanation, though a limited thing, can conceivably be an unbroken fabric so far as it goes—in other words, can, within the limits, be self-complete.

We might imagine ourselves locked in the system that natural science and history fasten around us if there were not one glaring hole in the screen—a hole which nobody can ever pretend to patch up. There is something which is closer to us, more intimate, more real, more direct, than all the external evidence in the world. The only thing in the universe which any of us can know in any sense from the inside is a single personality—namely, himself; and only from an internal knowledge of ourselves can we begin to build up our impressions of other people. The primary judgment that any of us makes, anterior to all philosophising and all scientific endeavour, is a judgment that conditions all other judgments—namely a judgment that we make about ourselves. The historian, in this particular sense, does not regard personality as a mere "thing", to be studied as other external things are studied. At this point, as we shall see, he rises above what are generally regarded as the ordinary methods of science.

It may be suggested that, though religious men have been inconceivably unwise on so many occasions, the Christian who adopts the view of the scientific method that has been described is in a position to hold his mind more free for hypothesis than those who seek from science their over-all view of life and the universe. It is the Marxists and the secularist systematisers of our time who, without reaching as high as God and without confining themselves to necessary inferences from observed phenomena, commit their minds to vast intermediate systems of ideas—systems which are less capable of elasticity than science itself demands, and which control the range of hypothesis sometimes, or constrict the adventures of the mind, since they create their own demand for conservatism and consistency . . . The believer in Providence can be prepared for any surprises. The Christian need put no limits to the Creator's versatility. . . .

Large areas of [history] are less capable of reduction to regularity or law than many people would seem to wish.

The kind of history which has developed in our civilisation and was handed down to the twentieth century has clustered around personalities and we have tended to think of it as organising itself into the form of narrative. It resurrects particular periods, reconstitutes particular episodes, follows the fortunes and discusses the decisions of individual people, and rejoices to recover the past in its concreteness and particularity. It does not limit its interests to the things that can be reduced to law and necessity—a project more feasible to those who direct their studies upon the materialistic side of human beings and human purpose. It is more interested in what is free, varied and unpredictable in the actions of individuals; and the higher realms of human activity—the art and the spiritual life of men—are not inessentials, not a mere fringe to the story. The play of personality itself is not a mere ornament in any case—not a kind of cadenza or violin obligato—but is itself a factor in the fundamental structure of history. The historical process is so flexible that all the future would have been different in a way that it is beyond the power of our mathematics to calculate if Napoleon had been shot in his youth or Hitler had failed in January, 1933. In this sense history is like life and every individual should be aware that it does really matter to the world what decision he makes on a given issue here and now.

Now, this attitude to the study of the past, if it is not to some degree the effect of our traditions—our Christian civilisation, with its high view of personality—is particularly congenial to those traditions and particularly appropriate for the Christian. It implies a telling of the story which has the effect of doing justice to freedom as well as necessity, and in which the spiritual (as well as the material) is organic to the theme—not a mere added ornament. It is typified in the flexibility of narrative, and is to be contrasted with the kind of history which sets out rather to schematise the centuries or turn everything into a process. The traditional historian has shown an interest in individuals for their own sake, and in a bygone generation as an end in itself, which we in our civilisation have perhaps too easily taken for granted. It is possible that a grossly materialistic civilisation, too intent upon utilitarian purposes, would not see the point of these things and would not produce the kind of fabric that we call history. The Christian must defend it however; for this is a kind of history in which—in a certain sense at least—personalities are the irreducible things.

Our traditional historical writing has gone further than this. It has refused to be satisfied with any merely casual or stand-offish attitude towards the personalities of the past. It does not treat them as mere things, or just measure such features of them as the scientist might measure; and its does not content itself with merely reporting about them in the way an external observer would do. It insists that the story cannot be told correctly unless we see the personalities from the inside, feeling with them as an actor might feel the part he is playing—thinking their thoughts over again and sitting in the position not of the observer but the doer of the action. If it is argued that this impossible—as indeed it is—not merely does it still remain the thing to aspire to, but in any case the historian must put himself in the place of the historical personage, must feel his predicament, must think as though he were that man. Without this art not only is it impossible to tell the story correctly but it is impossible to interpret the very documents on which the reconstruction depends. Traditional historical writing emphasises the importance of sympathetic imagination for the purpose of getting inside human beings. We may even say that this is part of the science of history for it produces communicable results—the insight of one historian may be ratified by scholars in general, who then give currency to the interpretation that is produced . . . The whole process of emptying oneself in order to catch the outlook and feelings of men not like-minded with oneself is an activity which ought to commend itself to the Christian. In this sense the whole range of history is a boundless field for the constant exercise of Christian charity.

At this point it becomes relevant to discuss the possibility of a Christian interpretation of history within the scheme of things which is now in question.

What we begin with is a form of historical scholarship restricted to a realm of tangible things, things which are to be established from concrete kinds of evidence. It is necessary to make inferences from the evidence and to have insights into personality, but the inferences and the insights belong to the same limited realm; they are, so to speak, very near to earth. In fact, we should expect them to be generally communicable, indeed to be ratified by a certain consensus of opinion, before the result could be accepted as a part of scholarship. In all this we may feel that we are studying the ways of Providence, but we cannot say that we have demonstrated the existence of Providence—we cannot say: "Here is evidence that ought to be sufficient to convince any neutral person". When we have reconstructed the past all that we have obtained is a picture of life as it must appear to any person living in the world; except that, whereas an individual only sees his three-score years and ten of it, he can now extend his vision and recognise certain long-term processes and tendencies.

If in life a man has accepted the Christian view of things, he will run these values throughout the whole story of the past, and, taking the very basis of narrative which historical scholarship has provided, he may see every event with an added dimension. He will have used historical science in order to become a closer and better student of the ways of Providence. He will see the vividness and appropriateness of the Biblical interpretation of history for the study of any country in any age of its history. He will not claim that historical science has demonstrated the truth of the interpretation which as a Christian he puts upon human events. His over-all view of things is partly dependent on the attitude that he brings to history in the first place; and partly it is dependent on the most intimate judgments that he makes about himself, about life as he has experienced it, and about the course of centuries as he has gathered it from historical scholarship. In this sense there is a Christian interpretation of the whole human drama, which is simply an interpretation of life—indeed, an aspect of the religion itself.

It is often assumed, however, that within the field of historical scholarship as we have described it, there is a Christian organisation which can be given to the narrative; in other words, that the European history which appears in our educational curriculum can be given such a form that it bears a Christian interpretation and vindicates the Church not merely in its spiritual functions but in its mundane policies. It soon becomes apparent that there has to be a Protestant history which is not only different from the Catholic version, but violently contradictory to it at times. Indeed, the attempt to vindicate Christianity in history easily turns into an attempt to justify Christians instead. . . .

Three things, however, seem to illustrate the importance of Christianity in . . . mundane history . . .—the importance of the particular religion which presided over the rise of what we call our Western civilisation. They all spring from the very nature of the Christian gospel itself. . . . They show that the Church has best served civilisation not on the occasions when it had civilisation as its conscious object, but when it was most intent on the salvation of souls and most content to leave the rest to Providence. The three things are the leavening effect of Christian charity, the assertion of the autonomy of spiritual principle, and the insistence on the spiritual character of personality. Apart from the softening effect that religion often (but perhaps not always) has had on manners and morals, these things have had their influences on the very texture of our Western civilisation. . . .

The ultimate vindication of the Christian religion in history, however, is not to be found in any of its mundane by-products, but in the spiritual life itself.

A Sceptical View of Historiography

René Descartes (1596–1650), the father of modern philosophy, was educated by the Jesuits. His favorite subject was mathematics "because of the certainty of its proofs and the evidence of its reasonings." In 1619 he dreamt of "a marvellous science" by which physics should be reduced to geometry and all sciences interconnected. Much of his life of "solitary intellectual passion," lived, as Etienne Gilson has said, "for the joy of knowing," was passed away from his native France in the relatively liberal atmosphere of Holland.

I did not fail . . . to esteem the exercises with which one is occupied in the schools. I knew that the languages one learns there are necessary for the understanding of ancient literature; that the charm of the fables awakens the mind; that the memorable actions of the histories elevate it and that, read with discretion, they help to form one's judgment; that the reading of all good books is like a conversation with the worthiest men of past centuries who were their authors, and, indeed, a studied conversation in which they reveal to us only their best thoughts.

[Descartes here enumerates the virtues of the study of eloquence, poetry, mathematics, morals, theology, philosophy, jurisprudence, medicine, and the other sciences.]

But I thought I had already given enough time to languages, and even also to reading the works of the ancients, both their histories and their fables. For to converse with men of other centuries is almost the same as to travel. It is good to know something of the customs of different peoples, in order to judge our own more soundly, and so that we do not think that everything which is contrary to our fashions is ridiculous and unreasonable, as those men customarily do who have seen nothing. But when one spends too much time in travelling, one becomes at last a stranger in one's own country; and when one is too curious about the practices of past centuries, one ordinarily remains very ignorant of the practices of this one. Besides which, fables make us conceive

From René Descartes, *Discours de la Méthode* in *Oeuvres de Descartes*, Vol. VI, ed. C. Adam and P. Tannery (Paris: L. Cerf, 1902). Translated for this volume by the editors.

as possible various events which are not so; and also the most accurate histories, if they neither change nor heighten the value of things, to make them more worthy of being read about, at least nearly always omit the basest and least illustrious circumstances: whence it comes that the remainder does not appear as it was, and that those who rule their conduct by the examples which they draw from histories, are apt to fall into the extravagances of the knights of our romances, and to conceive designs beyond their strength.

A New Conception of Historiography

Giambattista Vico (1668–1744) lived all his life in or near Naples, where he held the ill-paid post of professor of rhetoric from 1699 to 1741. Charitable and trusting, he was disappointed in his hopes of patronage and preferment. His works, particularly the Universal Law *(1721–1722) and* The New Science *(first edition 1725, revised editions 1730 and 1744) won him some honor, though little understanding. His* Autobiography *(trans. M. H. Fisch and T. G. Bergin, Ithaca, N.Y.: Cornell University Press, 1944) describes his intellectual development.*

[THE PRINCIPLES AND NATURE
OF THE "NEW SCIENCE"]

331 . . . In the night of thick darkness enveloping the earliest antiquity, so remote from ourselves, there shines the eternal and never-failing light of a truth beyond all question: that the world of civil society has certainly been made by men, and that its principles are therefore to be found within the modifications of our own human mind. Whoever reflects on this cannot but marvel that the philosophers should have bent all their energies to the study of the world of nature, which, since God made it, He alone knows; and that they should have neglected the study of the world of nations or civil world, which, since men had made it, men could hope to know. . . .

332 Now since this world of nations has been made by men, let us see in what things all men agree and always have agreed. For these things will be able to give us the universal and eternal principles (such as every science must have) on which all nations were founded and still preserve themselves.

333 We observe that all nations, barbarous as well as civilized, though separately founded because remote from each other in time and space, keep these three human customs: all have some religion, all contract solemn marriages, all bury their dead. And in

From *The New Science of Giambattista Vico* (translated from the 3d ed. of 1744 T. G. Bergin and M. H. Fisch; Ithaca, N.Y.: Cornell University Press, 1948), pp. 56–57, 70–71, 85–94, 382–383, *passim.* Copyright, 1948, by Cornell University, used with permission of Cornell University Press.

no nation, however savage and crude, are any human activities celebrated with more elaborate ceremonies and more sacred solemnity than religion, marriage and burial. For, by the axiom that "uniform ideas, born among peoples unknown to each other, must have a common ground of truth," it must have been dictated to all nations that from these three institutions humanity began among them all, and therefore they must be most devoutly observed by them all, so that the world should not again become a bestial wilderness. For this reason we have taken these three eternal and universal customs as three first principles of this Science.

334 Let not our first principle be accused of falsehood by the modern travelers who narrate that peoples of Brazil, South Africa and other nations of the new world live in society without any knowledge of God, as Antoine Arnauld believes to be the case also of the inhabitants of the islands called Antilles. Persuaded perhaps by them, Bayle affirms in his treatise on comets that peoples can live in justice without the light of God. This is a bolder statement than Polybius ventured in the dictum for which he has been acclaimed, that if the world had philosophers, living in justice by reason and not by laws, it would have no need of religions. These are travelers' tales, to promote the sale of their books by the narration of portents. . . . For all nations believe in a provident divinity, yet through all the length of years and all the breadth of this civil world it has been possible to find only four primary religions. The first is that of the Hebrews, whence came that of the Christians, both believing in the divinity of an infinite free mind. The third is that of the gentiles, who believe in the divinity of a plurality of gods, each imagined as composed of body and of free mind. Hence, when they wish to signify the divinity that rules and preserves the world, they speak of *deos immortales*. The fourth and last is that of the Mohammedans, who believe in the divinity of one god, an infinite free mind in an infinite body, for they look forward to pleasures of the senses as rewards in the other life. . . .

336 In the second place, the opinion that the sexual unions which certainly take place between free men and free women without solemn matrimony are free of natural wickedness [i.e. do not offend the law of nature], all the nations of the world have branded as false by the human customs with which they all religiously celebrate marriages, thereby determining that this sin is bestial, though in

venial degree. And for this reason: such parents, since they are held together by no necessary bond of law, are bound to abandon their natural children. Since their parents may separate at any time, if they are abandoned by both, the children must lie exposed to be devoured by dogs. If humanity, public or private, does not bring them up, they will have to grow up with no one to teach them religion, language, or any other human custom. . . .

337 Finally, [to realize] what a great principle of humanity burial is, imagine a feral state in which human bodies remain unburied on the surface of the earth as food for crows and dogs. Certainly this bestial custom will be accompanied by uncultivated fields and uninhabited cities. Men will go about like swine eating the acorns found amidst the putrefaction of their dead. And so with good reason burials were characterized by the sublime phrase "compacts of the human race" (*foedera generis humani*), and with less grandeur were described by Tacitus as "fellowships of humanity" (*humanitatis commercia*). . . .

338 To complete the establishment of the principles which have been adopted for this Science, it remains . . . to discuss the method which it should follow. It must begin where its subject matter began . . . Our treatment of it must take its start from the time these creatures began to think humanly. In their monstrous savagery and unbridled bestial freedom there was no means to tame the former or bridle the latter but the frightful thought of some divinity, the fear of whom . . . is the only powerful means of reducing to duty a liberty gone wild. To discover the way in which this first human thinking arose in the gentile world, we encountered exasperating difficulties which have cost us the research of a good twenty years. [We had] to descend from these human and refined natures of ours to those quite wild and savage natures, which we cannot at all imagine and can apprehend only with great effort.

339 By reason of all this, we must start from some notion of God such as even the most savage, wild and monstrous men do not lack. That notion we show to be this: that man, fallen into despair of all the succors of nature, desires something superior to save him. But something superior to nature is God, and this is the light that God has shed on all men. Confirmation may be found in a common human custom, that libertines grown old, feeling their natural forces fail, turn naturally to religion. . . .

341 But men because of their corrupted nature are under the tyranny of self-love, which compels them to make private utility their chief guide. Seeking everything useful for themselves and nothing for their companions, they cannot bring their passions under control to direct them toward justice. We thereby establish the fact that man in the bestial state desires only his own welfare; having taken wife and begotten children, he desires his own welfare along with that of his family; having entered upon civil life, he desires his own welfare along with that of his city; when its rule is extended over several peoples, he desires his own welfare along with that of the nation; when the nations are united by wars, treaties of peace, alliances and commerce, he desires his own welfare along with that of the entire human race. In all these conditions man desires principally his own utility. Therefore it is only by divine providence that he can be held within these orders to practice justice as a member of the society of the family, the state, and finally of mankind. Unable to attain all the utilities he wishes, he is constrained by these orders to seek those which are his due; and this is called just. That which regulates all human justice is therefore divine justice, which is administered by divine providence to preserve human society.

342 In one of its principal aspects, this Science must therefore be a rational civil theology of divine providence, which seems hitherto to have been lacking. . . . Our new Science must therefore be a demonstration, so to speak, of the historical fact of providence, for it must be a history of the forms of order which, without human discernment or intent, and often against the designs of men, providence has given to this great city of the human race. For though this world has been created in time and particular, the orders established therein by providence are universal and eternal. . . .

[THE IDEAL ETERNAL HISTORY OF EVERY NATION]

238 The order of ideas must follow the order of things.

LXV

239 This was the order of human things: first the forests, after that the huts, thence the villages, next the cities and finally the academies. . . .

LXVI

241 Men first feel necessity, then look for utility, next attend to comfort, still later amuse themselves with pleasure, thence grow dissolute in luxury, and finally go mad and waste their substance.

XLVII

242 The nature of peoples is first crude, then severe, then benign, then delicate, finally dissolute.

LXVIII

243 In the human race first appear the huge and grotesque, like the cyclopes; then the proud and magnanimous, like Achilles; then the valorous and just, like Aristedes and Scipio Africanus; nearer to us, imposing figures with great semblances of virtue accompanied by great vices, who among the vulgar win a name for true glory, like Alexander and Caesar; still later, the melancholy and reflective, like Tiberius; finally the dissolute and shameless madmen, like Caligula, Nero, and Domitian.

244 This axiom shows that the first sort were necessary in order to make one man obey another in the family-state and prepare him to be law-abiding in the city-state that was to come; the second sort, who naturally did not yield to their peers, were necessary to establish the aristocratic commonwealths on the basis of the families; the third sort to open the way for popular liberty; the fourth to bring in the monarchies; the fifth to establish them; the sixth to overthrow them.

245 This with the preceding axioms [LXV–LXVII] gives a part of the principles of the ideal eternal history traversed in time by every nation in its rise, development, maturity, decline and fall. . . .

345 . . . The proper and consecutive proof here adduced will consist in comparing and reflecting whether our human mind, in the series of possibilities it is permitted to understand, and so far as it is permitted to do so, can conceive more or fewer or different causes than those from which issue the effects of this civil world. In doing this the reader will experience in his mortal body a divine pleasure as he contemplates in the divine ideas this world of nations in all the extent of its places, times and varieties. And he will find that he has in effect convinced the Epicureans that their chance cannot wander foolishly about and everywhere find a way out, and the Stoics that their eternal chain of causes, to which

they will have it the world is chained, itself hangs upon the omnipotent, wise and beneficent will of the best and greatest God. . . .

347 In search of these natures of human things our Science proceeds by a severe analysis of human thoughts about the human necessities or utilities of social life, which are the two perennial springs of the natural law of nations . . . In its second principal aspect, our Science is therefore a history of human ideas, on which it seems the metaphysics of the human mind must proceed. This queen of the sciences, by the axiom that "the sciences must begin where their subject matters began," took its start when the first men began to think humanly, and not when the philosophers began to reflect on human ideas. . . .

349 Our Science therefore comes to describe at the same time an ideal eternal history traversed in time by the history of every nation in its rise, progress, maturity, decline and fall. Indeed we go so far as to assert that whoever meditates this Science tells himself this ideal eternal history only so far as he makes it by that proof "it had, has, and will have to be." For the first indubitable principle above posited is that this world of nations has certainly been made by men, and its guise must therefore be found within the modifications of our own human mind. And history cannot be more certain than when he who creates the things also describes them. Thus our Science proceeds exactly as does geometry, which, while it constructs out of its elements or contemplates the world of quantity, itself creates it; but with a reality greater in proportion to that of the orders having to do with human affairs, in which there are neither points, lines, surfaces, nor figures. And this very fact is an argument, O reader, that these proofs are of a kind divine, and should give thee a divine pleasure; since in God knowledge and creation are one and the same thing. . . .

[PHILOSOPHICAL METHOD]

137 Men who do not know the truth of things try to reach certainty about them, so that, if they cannot satisfy their intellects by science, their wills at least may rest on conscience.

x

138 Philosophy contemplates reason, whence comes knowledge of the true; philology observes the authority of human choice, whence comes consciousness of the certain.

139   This axiom by its second part defines as philologians all the grammarians, historians, critics, who have occupied themselves with the study of the languages and deeds of peoples: both their domestic affairs, such as customs and laws, and their external affairs, such as wars, peaces, alliances, travels and commerce.

140   This same axiom shows how the philosophers failed by half in not giving certainty to their reasonings by appeal to the authority of the philologians, and likewise how the latter failed by half in not taking care to give their authority the sanction of truth by appeal to the reasoning of the philosophers. If they had both done this they would have been more useful to their commonwealths and they would have anticipated us in conceiving this Science. . . .

[PHILOLOGICAL METHOD]

351   These are the philosophic proofs our Science will use, and consequently those which are absolutely necessary for pursuing it. The philological proofs must come last. They all reduce to the following kinds:

352   First, that our mythologies agree with the results of our meditations, not by force and distortion, but directly, easily and naturally; that they will be seen to be civil histories of the first peoples, who are everywhere found to have been naturally poets.

353   Second, that the heroic phrases, as here explained in the full truth of the sentiments and the full propriety of the expressions, also agree.

354   Third, that the etymologies of the native languages also agree, which tell us the histories of the things signified by the words, beginning with their original and proper meanings and pursuing the natural progress of their metaphors according to the order of the ideas, on which the history of languages must proceed. . . .

355   Fourth, the mental vocabulary of human social things, which are the same in substance as felt by all nations but diversely expressed in language according to their diverse manifestations, is exhibited to be such as we conceived it in the Axioms.[1]

356   Fifth, truth is sifted from falsehood in everything that has been preserved for us through long centuries by those vulgar traditions which, since they have been preserved for so long a time

---

[1] That is, "a mental language common to all nations," *New Science*, p. 160.—Ed.

and by entire peoples, must . . . have had a public ground of truth.

357   Sixth, the great fragments of antiquity, hitherto useless to science because they lay neglected, broken and scattered, shed great light when cleaned, pieced together and set in place.

358   Seventh and last, to all these things, as to their necessary causes, are assigned all the effects narrated by certain history.

359   These philological proofs enable us to see in fact the things we have meditated in idea concerning this world of nations, in accordance with Bacon's method of philosophizing, which is "think [and] see" (*cogitare videre*). Thus it is that with the help of the preceding philosophical proofs, the philological proofs which follow both confirm their own authority by reason and at the same time confirm reason by their authority.

360   From all that has been set forth in general concerning the establishment of the principles of this Science, we conclude that, since its principles are divine providence, moderation of the passions by marriage, and immortality of human souls [witnessed] by burial, and since the criterion it uses is that what is felt to be just by all men or by the majority must be the rule of social life (and on these principles and this criterion there is agreement between the vulgar wisdom of all lawgivers and the esoteric wisdom of the philosophers of greatest repute), these must be the bounds of human reason. And let him who would transgress them beware lest he transgress all humanity. . . .

[C O N C L U S I O N]
1108   It is true that men have themselves made this world of nations (and we took this as the first incontestable principle of our Science, since we despaired of finding it from the philosophers and philologists), but this world without doubt has issued from a mind often diverse, at times quite contrary, and always superior to the particular ends that men had proposed to themselves; which narrow ends, made means to serve wider ends, it has always employed to preserve the human race upon this earth. Men mean to gratify their bestial lust and abandon their offspring, and they inaugurate the chastity of marriage from which the families arise. The fathers mean to exercise without restraint their paternal power over their clients, and they subject them to the civil powers from which the cities arise. The reigning orders of nobles mean to

abuse their lordly freedom over the plebeians, and they are obliged to submit to the laws which establish popular liberty. The free peoples mean to shake off the yoke of their laws, and they become subject to monarchs. The monarchs mean to strengthen their own positions by debasing their subjects with all the vices of dissoluteness, and they dispose them to endure slavery at the hands of stronger nations. The nations mean to dissolve themselves, and their remnants flee for safety to the wilderness, whence, like the phoenix, they rise again. That which did all this was mind, for men did it with intelligence; it was not fate, for they did it by choice; not chance, for the results of their always so acting are perpetually the same.

1109 . . . In this work it has been fully demonstrated that through providence the first governments of the world had as their entire form religion, on which alone the state of the families was based; and passing thence to the heroic or aristocratic civil governments, religion must have been their principal firm basis. Advancing then to the popular governments, it was again religion that served the peoples as means for attaining them. And coming to rest at last in monarchic governments, this same religion must be the shield of princes. Hence, if religion is lost among the peoples, they have nothing left to enable them to live in society: no shield of defense, nor means of counsel, nor basis of support, nor even a form by which they may exist in the world at all.

G. W. F. HEGEL

Philosophical Historiography

Georg Wilhelm Friedrich Hegel (1770–1831), after a career as private tutor, headmaster, and professor, in 1818 became professor of philosophy at Berlin. There, although he was an awkward lecturer, a school gathered round him. In 1807 his Phenomenology of Mind *appeared; in 1812 and 1816 the two parts of the* Science of Logic; *and in 1821,* The Philosophy of Right. *His* Philosophy of History, *from which the following extracts are taken, was reconstituted for publication from students' notes of his Berlin lectures. His influence has been various, affecting historians and classical scholars as well as philosophers, and communists as well as existentialists.*

[THE PRESUPPOSITIONS OF PHILOSOPHICAL HISTORY]

The most general definition that can be given, is, that the Philosophy of History means nothing but the *thoughtful consideration of it*. Thought is, indeed, essential to humanity. It is this that distinguishes us from the brutes. In sensation, cognition, and intellection; in our instincts and volitions, as far as they are truly human, Thought is an invariable element. To insist upon Thought in this connection with history may, however, appear unsatisfactory. In this science it would seem as if Thought must be subordinate to what is given, to the realities of fact; that this is its basis and guide: while Philosophy dwells in the region of self-produced ideas, without reference to actuality. Approching history thus prepossessed, Speculation might be expected to treat it as a mere passive material; and, so far from leaving it in its native truth, to force it into conformity with a tyrannous idea, and to construe it, as the phrase is, "*à priori*." But as it is the business of history simply to adopt into its records what is and has been, actual occurrences and transactions; and since it remains true to its character in proportion as it strictly adheres to its data, we seem to have in Philosophy, a process diametrically opposed to that of the historiographer. This contradiction, and the charge consequently brought against speculation, shall be explained and confuted . . .

From G. W. F. Hegel, *The Philosophy of History*, trans. J. Sibree (New York: Dover Publications, Inc., 1956), pp. 8–39.

The only Thought which Philosophy brings with it to the contemplation of History, is the simple conception of *Reason;* that Reason is the Sovereign of the World; that the history of the world, therefore, presents us with a rational process. This conviction and intuition is a hypothesis in the domain of history as such. In that of Philosophy it is no hypothesis. It is there proved by speculative cognition, that Reason—and this term may here suffice us, without investigating the relation sustained by the Universe to the Divine Being—is *Substance,* as well as *Infinite Power;* its own *Infinite Material* underlying all the natural and spiritual life which it originates, as also the *Infinite Form*—that which sets this Material in motion . . . While it is exclusively its own basis of existence, and absolute final aim, it is also the energizing power realizing this aim; developing it not only in the phenomena of the Natural, but also of the Spiritual Universe—the History of the World. That this "Idea" or "Reason" is the *True,* the *Eternal,* the absolutely *powerful* essence; that it reveals itself in the World, and that in that World nothing else is revealed but this and its honor and glory—is the thesis which, as we have said, has been proved in Philosophy, and is here regarded as demonstrated . . .

If the clear idea of Reason is not already developed in our minds, in beginning the study of Universal History, we should at least have the firm, unconquerable faith that Reason *does* exist there . . . Yet I am not obliged to make any such preliminary demand upon your faith. What I have said thus provisionally, and what I shall have further to say, is, even in reference to *our* branch of science, not to be regarded as hypothetical, but as a summary view of the whole; the *result of the investigation* we are about to pursue; a result which happens to be known to *me,* because I have traversed the entire field . . . We have . . . to mention here:

(1) The abstract characteristics of the nature of Spirit.

(2) What means Spirit uses in order to realize its Idea.

(3) Lastly, we must consider the shape which the perfect embodiment of Spirit assumes—the State.

[THE ABSTRACT CHARACTERISTICS OF SPIRIT]

The nature of Spirit may be understood by a glance at its direct opposite—*Matter.* As the essence of Matter is Gravity, so, on the other hand, we may affirm that the substance, the essence of Spirit is Freedom. All will readily assent to the doctrine that Spirit, among other properties, is also endowed with Freedom; but philosophy teaches that all the qualities of Spirit exist only through Freedom; that all are but means for attaining Freedom; that all seek and produce this and this alone. It is a result of speculative Philosophy, that Freedom is the sole truth of Spirit . . . Spirit is *self-contained existence* (Bei-sich-selbst-seyn). Now this is Freedom, exactly. For if I am dependent, my being is referred to something else which I am not; I cannot exist independently of something external. I am free, on the contrary, when my existence depends upon myself. This self-contained existence of Spirit is none other than self-consciousness—consciousness of one's own being. Two things must be distinguished in consciousness; first, the fact *that I know;* secondly, *what I know.* In *self* consciousness these are merged in one; for Spirit *knows itself.* It involves an appreciation of its own nature, as also an energy enabling it to realize itself; to make itself *actually* that which it is *potentially.* According to this abstract definition it may be said of Universal History, that it is the exhibition of Spirit in the process of working out the knowledge of that which it is potentially. And as the germ bears in itself the whole nature of the tree, and the taste and form of its fruits, so do the first traces of Spirit virtually contain the whole of that History. The Orientals have not attained the knowledge that Spirit—Man *as such*—is free; and because they do not know this, they are not free. They only know that *one is free.* But on this very account, the freedom of that one is only caprice; ferocity— brutal recklessness of passion, or a mildness and tameness of the desires, which is itself only an accident of Nature—mere caprice like the former.—That *one* is therefore only a Despot; not a *free man.* The consciousness of Freedom first arose among the Greeks, and therefore they were free; but they, and the Romans likewise, knew only that *some* are free—not man as such. Even Plato and Aristotle did not know this. The Greeks, therefore, had slaves; and their whole life and the maintenance of their splendid liberty, was implicated with the institution of slavery: a fact moreover, which made that liberty on the one hand only an accidental, transient and limited growth; on the other hand, constituted it a rigorous thraldom of our common nature—of the Human. The German nations, under the influence of Christianity, were the first to attain the consciousness, that man, as man, is free: that it is the *freedom* of Spirit which constitutes its essence. This consciousness arose first in religion, the inmost region of Spirit; but to introduce the principle into the various relations of the actual world, involves a more extensive problem than its simple implantation; a problem whose solution and application require a severe and lengthened process of culture. In proof of this, we may note that slavery did not cease immediately on the reception of Christianity. Still less did liberty predominate in States; or Governments and Constitutions adopt a rational organization, or recognize freedom as their basis. That application of the principle to political relations; the thorough moulding and interpenetration of the constitution of society by it, is a process identical with history itself. I have already directed attention to the distinction here involved, between a principle as such, and its *application; i.e.,* its introduction and carrying out in the actual phenomena of Spirit and Life. This is a point of fundamental importance in our science, and one which must be constantly respected as essential. And in the same way as this distinction has attracted attention in view of the *Christian* principle of self-consciousness—Freedom; it also shows itself as an essential one, in view of the principle of Freedom *generally*. The History of the world is none other than the progress of the consciousness of Freedom; a progress whose development according to the necessity of its nature, it is our business to investigate.

The general statement given above, of the various grades in the consciousness of Freedom—and which we applied in the first instance to the fact that the Eastern nations knew only that *one* is free; the Greek and Roman world only that *some* are free; while *we* know that all men absolutely (man *as man*) are free—supplies us with the natural division of Universal History, and suggests the mode of its discussion. . . .

[THE MEANS BY WHICH SPIRIT REALIZES ITS IDEA]

The question of the *means* by which Freedom develops itself to a World, conducts us to the phenomenon of History itself. Although Freedom is, primarily, an undeveloped idea, the means it uses are external and phenomenal; presenting themselves in History to our sensuous vision. The first glance at History convinces us that the actions of men proceed from their needs, their passions, their characters and talents; and impresses us with the belief that such needs, passions and interests are the sole springs of action—the efficient agents in this scene of activity. Among these may, perhaps, be found aims of a liberal or universal kind—benevolence it may be, or noble patriotism; but such virtues and general views are but insignificant as compared with the World and its doings. We may perhaps see the Ideal of Reason actualized in those who adopt such aims, and within the sphere of their influence; but they bear only a trifling proportion to the mass of the human race; and the extent of that influence is limited accordingly. Passions, private aims, and the satisfaction of selfish desires, are on the other hand, most effective springs of action. Their power lies in the fact that they respect none of the limitations which justice and morality would impose on them; and that these natural impulses have a more direct influence over man than the artificial and tedious discipline that tends to order and self-restraint, law and morality. When we look at this display of passions, and the consequences of their violence; the Unreason which is associated not only with them, but even (rather we might say *especially*) with *good* designs and righteous aims; when we see the evil, the vice, the ruin that has befallen the most flourishing kingdoms which the mind of man ever created; we can scarce avoid being filled with sorrow at this universal taint of corruption: and, since this decay is not the work of mere Nature, but of the Human Will—a moral embitterment—a revolt of the Good Spirit (if it have a place within us) may well be the result of our reflections . . . We endure in beholding it a mental torture, allowing no defence or escape but the consideration that what has happened could not be otherwise; that it is a fatality which no intervention could alter . . . But even regarding History as the slaughter-bench at which the happiness of peoples, the wisdom of States, and the virtue of individuals have been victimized—the question involuntarily arises—to what principle, to what final aim these enormous sacrifices have been offered . . .

The *first* remark we have to make, and which—though already presented more than once—cannot be too often repeated when the occasion seems to call for it—is that what we call *principle, aim, destiny,* or the nature and idea of Spirit, is something merely general and abstract. Principle—Plan of Existence—Law—is a hidden, undeveloped essence, which *as such*—however true in itself—is not completely real. Aims, principles, etc., have a place in our thoughts, in our subjective design only; but not yet in the sphere of reality.

That which exists for itself only, is a possibility, a potentiality; but has not yet emerged into Existence. A *second* element must be introduced in order to produce actuality—viz., actuation, realization; and whose motive power is the Will—the activity of man in the widest sense. It is only by this activity that that Idea as well as abstract characteristics generally, are realized, actualized; for of themselves they are powerless. The motive power that puts them in operation, and gives them determinate existence, is the need, instinct, inclination, and passion of man . . .

We assert then that nothing has been accomplished without interest on the part of the actors; and—if interest be called passion, inasmuch as the whole individuality, to the neglect of all other actual or possible interests and claims, is devoted to an object with every fibre of volition, concentrating all its desires and powers upon it—we may affirm absolutely that *nothing great in the World* has been accomplished without *passion.* Two elements, therefore, enter into the object of our investigation; the first the Idea, the second the complex of human passions; the one the warp, the other the woof of the vast arras-web of Universal History. The concrete mean and union of the two is Liberty, under the conditions of morality in a State. We have spoken of the Idea of Freedom as the nature of Spirit, and the absolute goal of History . . .

From this comment on the second essential element in the historical embodiment of an aim, we infer—glancing at the institution of the State in passing—that a State is then well constituted and internally powerful, when the private interest of its citizens is one with the common interest of the State; when the one finds its gratification and realization in the other—a proposition in itself very important. But in a State many institutions must be adopted, much political machinery invented, accompanied by appropriate political arrangements—necessitating long struggles of the understanding before what is really appropriate can be discovered—involving, moreover, contentions with private interest and passions, and a tredious discipline of these latter, in order to bring about the desired harmony. The epoch when a State attains this harmonious condition, marks the period of its bloom, its virtue, its vigor, and its prosperity. But the history of mankind does not begin with a *conscious* aim of any kind, as it is the case with the particular circles into which men form themselves of set purpose . . .

An additional result is commonly produced by human actions

beyond that which they aim at and obtain—that which they immediately recognize and desire. They gratify their own interest; but something further is thereby accomplished, latent in the actions in question, though not present to their consciousness, and not included in their design. . . .

[WORLD-HISTORICAL INDIVIDUALS]

Caesar, in danger of losing a position, not perhaps at that time of superiority, yet at least of equality with the others who were at the head of the State, and of succumbing to those who were just on the point of becoming his enemies—belongs essentially to [the] category [of world-historical individuals] . . . These enemies—who were at the same time pursuing *their* personal aims—had the form of the constitution, and the power conferred by an appearance of justice, on their side. Caesar was contending for the maintenance of his position, honor, and safety; and, since the power of his opponents included the sovereignty over the provinces of the Roman Empire, his victory secured for him the conquest of that entire Empire; and he thus became—though leaving the form of the constitution—the Autocrat of the State. That which secured for him the execution of a design, which in the first instance was of negative import—the Autocracy of Rome—was, however, at the same time an independently necessary feature in the history of Rome and of the world. It was not, then, his private gain merely, but an unconscious impulse that occasioned the accomplishment of that for which the time was ripe. Such are all great historical men—whose own particular aims involve those large issues which are the will of the World-Spirit . . .

Such individuals had no consciousness of the general Idea they were unfolding, while prosecuting those aims of theirs; on the contrary, they were practical, political men. But at the same time they were thinking men, who had an insight into the requirements of the time—*what was ripe for development*. This was the very Truth for their age, for their world; the species next in order, so to speak, and which was already formed in the womb of time . . .

A World-historical individual is not so unwise as to indulge a variety of wishes to divide his regards. He is devoted to the One Aim, regardless of all else. It is even possible that such men may treat other great, even sacred interests, inconsiderately; conduct which is indeed obnoxious to moral reprehension. But so mighty a form must trample down many an innocent flower—crush to pieces many an object in its path.

The special interest of passion is thus inseparable from the active development of a general principle: for it is from the special and determinate and from its negation, that the Universal results. Particularity contends with its like, and some loss is involved in the issue. *It* is not the general idea that is implicated in opposition and combat, and that is exposed to danger. It remains in the background, untouched and uninjured. This may be called the *cunning of reason* —that it sets the passions to work for itself, while that which develops its existence through such impulsion pays the penalty, and suffers loss. For it is *phenomenal* being that is so treated, and of this, part is of no value, part is positive and real. The particular is for the most part of too trifling value as compared with the general: individuals are sacrificed and abandoned. The Idea pays the penalty of determinate existence and of corruptibility, not from itself, but from the passions of individuals. . . .

[THE STATE AS THE PERFECT EMBODIMENT OF SPIRIT]

What is the material in which the Ideal of Reason is wrought out? The primary answer would be—Personality itself—human desires—Subjectivity generally. In human knowledge and volition, as its material element, Reason attains positive existence . . . As a subjective will, occupied with limited passions, it is dependent, and can gratify its desires only within the limits of this dependence. But the subjective will has also a substantial life—a reality—in which it moves in the region of *essential* being, and has the essential itself as the object of its existence. This essential being is the union of the *subjective* with the *rational* Will: it is the moral Whole, the *State*, which is that form of reality in which the individual has and enjoys his freedom; but on the condition of his recognizing, believing in, and willing that which is common to the Whole. And this must not be understood as if the subjective will of the social unit attained its gratification and enjoyment through that common Will; as if this were a means provided for its benefit; as if the individual, in his relations to other individuals, thus limited his freedom, in order that this universal limitation—the mutual constraint of all—might secure a small space of liberty for each. Rather, we affirm, are Law, Morality, Government, and they alone, the positive reality and completion of Freedom. Freedom of a low and limited order, is mere caprice; which finds its exercise in the sphere of particular and limited desires.

Subjective volition—Passion—is that which sets men in activity, that which effects "practical" realization. The Idea is the inner spring of action; the State is the actually existing, realized moral life. For it is the Unity of the universal, essential Will, with that of the individual; and this is "Morality." The Individual living in this unity has a moral life; possesses a value that consists in this substantiality alone . . .

It is the absolute interest of Reason that this moral Whole should exist; and herein lies the justification and merit of heroes who have founded states—however rude these may have been. In the history of the World, only those peoples can come under our notice which form a state. For it must be understood that this latter is the realization of Freedom, *i.e.* of the absolute final aim, and that it exists for its own sake. It must further be understood that all the worth which the human being possesses—all spiritual reality, he possesses only through the State. For his spiritual reality consists in this, that his own essence—Reason—is objectively present to him, that it possesses objective immediate existence for him. Thus only is he fully conscious; thus only is he a partaker of morality— of a just and moral social and political life. For Truth is the Unity of the universal and subjective Will; and the Universal is to be found in the State, in its laws, its universal and rational arrangements. The State is the Divine Idea as it exists on Earth. We have in it, therefore, the object of History in a more definite shape than before; that in which Freedom obtains objectivity, and lives in the enjoyment of this objectivity. For Law is the objectivity of Spirit; volition in its true form. Only that will which obeys law, is free; for it obeys itself—it is independent and so free. When the State or our country constitutes a community of existence; when the subjective will of man submits to laws—the contradiction between Liberty and Necessity vanishes.

KARL MARX

The Materialist Conception of History

Karl Heinrich Marx (1818–1883), lived in exile and poverty, an apparent failure. Exiled from Germany for his radical political opinions and expelled from Paris and Brussels, he passed most of the last thirty-four years of his life in London. There his family's hardships were mitigated by the generosity of Friedrich Engels, whom Marx met in 1844 and who became his life-long friend and collaborator. Marx's most famous works are the Communist Manifesto *(1848, written with Engels) and* Capital *(first edition 1867), while an example of his own historical practice can be seen in* The Eighteenth Brumaire of Louis Bonaparte *(1852). Most of the following extracts are taken from Marx's lesser known writings of the 1840's, in which his mature ideas first emerged, but which also show the strength of his Hegelian background.*

[MARX'S SUMMARY OF HIS THOUGHT]
The general conclusion at which I arrived and which, once reached, continued to serve as the leading thread in my studies, may be briefly summed up as follows: In the social production which men carry on they enter into definite relations that are indispensable and independent of their will; these relations of production correspond to a definite stage of development of their material powers of production. The sum total of these relations of production constitutes the economic structure of society—the real foundation, on which rise legal and political superstructures and to which correspond definite forms of social consciousness. The mode of production in material life determines the general character of the social, political and spiritual processes of life. It is not the

The selections from Marx are taken from the following sources: *A Contribution to the Critique of Political Economy*, trans. N. I. Stone (Chicago: Charles H. Kerr, 1913), pp. 11–13; *Early Writings*, trans. & ed. T. B. Bottomore (London: C. A. Watts, 1963), pp. 21–26, and *Selected Writings in Sociology and Social Philosophy*, trans. T. B. Bottomore, eds. T. B. Bottomore and M. Rubel (London: C. A. Watts, 1956), pp. 231–233 (both reprinted by permission of C. A. Watts & Co., London); *Selected Essays*, trans. H. J. Stenning (New York: International Publishers, 1926), pp. 137–138; and Karl Marx and Friedrich Engels, *The German Ideology*, Parts I and III, ed. R. Pascal (New York: International Publishers, 1947), pp. 21–23, 28–29, 38–41 (used by permission of International Publishers Co., Inc.)

consciousness of men that determines their existence, but, on the contrary, their social existence determines their consciousness. At a certain stage of their development, the material forces of production in society come in conflict with the existing relations of production, or—what is but a legal expression for the same thing—with the property relations within which they had been at work before. From forms of development of the forces of production these relations turn into their fetters. Then comes the period of social revolution. With the change of the economic foundation the entire immense superstructure is more or less rapidly transformed. In considering such transformations the distinction should always be made between the material transformation of the economic conditions of production which can be determined with the precision of natural science, and the legal, political, religious, aesthetic or philosophic—in short ideological forms in which men become conscious of this conflict and fight it out. Just as our opinion of an individual is not based on what he thinks of himself, so can we not judge of such a period of transformation by its own consciousness; on the contrary, this consciousness must rather be explained from the contradictions of material life, from the existing conflict between the social forces of production and the relations of production. No social order ever disappears before all the productive forces, for which there is room in it, have been developed; and new higher relations of production never appear before the material conditions of their existence have matured in the womb of the old society. Therefore, mankind always takes up only such problems as it can solve since, looking at the matter more closely, we will always find that the problem itself arises only when the material conditions necessary for its solution already exist or are at least in the process of formation. In broad outlines we can designate the Asiatic, the ancient, the feudal, and the modern bourgeois methods of production as so many epochs in the progress of the economic formation of society. The bourgeois relations of production are the last antagonistic form of the social process of production—antagonistic not in the sense of individual antagonism, but of one arising from conditions surrounding the life of individuals in society; at the same time the productive forces developing in the womb of bourgeois society create the material conditions for the solution of that antagonism. This social formation constitutes, therefore, the closing chapter of the prehistoric stage of human society. [*Critique of Political Economy,* 1859]

[ALIENATED LABOR]

We shall begin from a *contemporary* economic fact. The worker becomes poorer the more wealth he produces and the more his production increases in power and extent. The worker becomes an ever cheaper commodity the more goods he creates. The *devaluation* of the human world increases in direct relation with the *increase in value* of the world of things. Labour does not only create goods; it also produces itself and the worker as a *commodity,* and indeed in the same proportion as it produces goods . . .

The worker is related to the *product of his labour* as to an *alien* object. For it is clear on this presupposition that the more the worker expends himself in work the more powerful becomes the world of objects which he creates in face of himself, the poorer he becomes in his inner life, and the less he belongs to himself. It is just the same as in religion. The more of himself man attributes to God the less he has left in himself. The worker puts his life into the object, and his life then belongs no longer to himself but to the object. The greater his activity, therefore, the less he possesses. What is embodied in the product of his labour is no longer his own. The greater this product is, therefore, the more he is diminished. The *alienation* of the worker in his product means not only that his labour becomes an object, assumes an *external* existence, but that it exists independently, *outside himself,* and alien to him, and that it stands opposed to him as an autonomous power. The life which he has given to the object sets itself against him as an alien and hostile force . . .

What constitutes the alienation of labour? First, that the work is *external* to the worker, that it is not part of his nature; and that, consequently, he does not fulfil himself in his work but denies himself, has a feeling of misery rather than well-being, does not develop freely his mental and physical energies but is physically exhausted and mentally debased. The worker, therefore, feels himself at home only during his leisure time, whereas at work he feels homeless. His work is not voluntary but imposed, *forced labour.* It is not the satisfaction of a need, but only a *means* for satisfying other needs. Its alien character is clearly shown by the fact that as soon as there is no physical or other compulsion it is avoided like the plague. External labour, labour in which man alienates himself, is a labour of self-sacrifice, of mortification. Finally, the external character of work for the worker is shown by the fact that it is not his own work but work for someone else, that in work he does not belong to himself but to another person.

Just as in religion the spontaneous activity of human fantasy, of the human brain and heart, reacts independently as an alien activity of gods or devils upon the individual, so the activity of the worker is not his own spontaneous activity. It is another's activity and a loss of his own spontaneity.

We arrive at the result that man (the worker) feels himself to be freely active only in his animal functions—eating, drinking and procreating, or at most also in his dwelling and in personal adornment—while in his human functions he is reduced to an animal. The animal becomes human and the human becomes animal.

Eating, drinking and procreating are of course also genuine human functions. But abstractly considered, apart from the environment of human activities, and turned into final and sole ends, they are animal functions. ["Economic and Philosophical Manuscripts," 1844, in *Early Writings*]

[DIVISION OF LABOR]

With the division of labour, . . . which in its turn is based on the natural division of labour in the family and the separation of society into individual families opposed to one another, is given simultaneously the distribution, and indeed the unequal distribution (both quantitative and qualitative), of labour and its products, hence property: the nucleus, the first form, of which lies in the family, where wife and children are the slaves of the husband. This latent slavery in the family, though still very crude, is the first property, but even at this early stage it corresponds perfectly to the definition of modern economists who call it the power of disposing of the labour-power of others. Division of labour and private property are, moreover, identical expressions: in the one the same thing is affirmed with reference to activity as is affirmed in the other with reference to the product of the activity.

Further, the division of labour implies the contradiction between the interest of the separate individual or the individual family and the communal interest of all individuals who have intercourse with one another. And indeed, this communal interest does not exist merely in the imagination, as "the general good," but first of all in reality, as the mutual interdependence of the individuals among whom the labour is divided. And finally, the division of labour offers us the first example of how, as long as man remains in natural society, that is as long as a cleavage exists between the particular and the common interest, as long therefore as activity is not voluntarily, but naturally, divided, man's own deed becomes an alien power opposed to him, which enslaves him instead of being controlled by him. For as soon as labour is distributed, each man has a particular, exclusive sphere of activity, which is forced upon him and from which he cannot escape. He is a hunter, a fisherman, a shepherd, or a critical critic, and must remain so if he does not want to lose his means of livelihood; while in communist society, where nobody has one exclusive sphere of activity but each can become accomplished in any branch he wishes, society regulates the general production and thus makes it possible for me to do one thing to-day and another to-morrow, to hunt in the morning, fish in the afternoon, rear cattle in the evening, criticize after dinner, just as I have a mind, without ever becoming hunter, fisherman, shepherd or critic.

This crystallization of social activity, this consolidation of what we ourselves produce into an objective power above us, growing out of our control, thwarting our expectations, bringing to naught our calculations, is one of the chief factors in historical development up till now. And out of this very contradiction between the interest of the individual and that of the community the latter takes an independent form as the STATE, divorced from the real interests of individual and community, and at the same time as an illusory communal life, always based, however, on the real ties existing in every family and tribal conglomeration (such as flesh and blood, language, division of labour on a larger scale, and other interests) and especially, as we shall enlarge upon later, on the classes, already determined by the division of labour, which in every such mass of men separate out, and of which one dominates all the others. It follows from this that all struggles within the State, the struggle between democracy, aristocracy and monarchy, the struggle for the franchise, etc., etc., are merely the illusory forms in which the real struggles of the different classes are fought out among one another. [*German Ideology*, 1845–46]

[THE PROLETARIAT AND BEYOND]

Proletariat and wealth are antinomies. As such they form a whole. They are two forms of the world of private property . . .

The possessing class and the proletarian class express the same human alienation. But the former is satisfied with its situation, feels itself well established in it, recognizes this self-alienation as *its own* power, and thus has the *appearance* of a human existence. The latter feels itself crushed by this self-alienation, sees in it its own impotence and the reality of an inhuman situation. . . .

Within the framework of alienation, therefore, the property owners are the *conservative* and the proletarians the *destructive* party.

It is true that, in its economic development, private property advances towards its own dissolution; but it only does this through a development which is independent of itself, unconscious and achieved against its will—solely because it produces the proletariat *as* proletariat, poverty conscious of its moral and physical poverty, degradation conscious of its degradation, and for this reason trying to abolish itself. The proletariat carries out the sentence which private property, by creating the proletariat, passes upon itself, just as it carries out the sentence which wage-labour, by creating wealth for others and poverty for itself, passes upon itself. If the proletariat triumphs this does not mean that it becomes the absolute form of society, for it is only victorious by abolishing itself as well as its opposite. Thus the proletariat disappears along with the opposite which conditions it, private property.

If socialist writers attribute this world-historical role to the proletariat this is not at all . . . because they regard the proletarians as *gods*. On the contrary, in the fully developed proletariat, everything human is taken away, even the *appearance* of humanity. In the conditions of existence of the proletariat are condensed, in their most inhuman form, all the conditions of existence of present-day society. Man has lost himself, but he has not only acquired, at the same time, a theoretical consciousness of his loss, he has been forced, by an ineluctable, irremediable and imperious *distress*—by practical *necessity*—to revolt against this inhumanity. It is for these reasons that the proletariat can and must emancipate itself. But it can only emancipate itself by destroying its own conditions of existence. It can only destroy its own conditions of existence by destroying *all* the inhuman conditions of existence of present-day society, conditions which are epitomized in its situation. It is not in vain that it passes through the rough but stimulating school of *labour*. It is not a matter of knowing what this or that proletarian, or even the proletariat as a whole, *conceives* as its aims at any particular moment. It is a question of knowing *what* the proletariat *is*, and what it must historically accomplish in accordance with its *nature*. Its aim and its historical activity are ordained for it, in a tangible and irrevocable way, by its own situation as well as by the whole organization of present-day civil society. [*The Holy Family*, 1845]

[HISTORY AND CIVIL SOCIETY]

Our conception of history depends on our ability to expound the real process of production, starting out from the simple material production of life, and to comprehend the form of intercourse connected with this and created by this (i.e. civil society in its various stages), as the basis of all history; further, to show it in its action as State; and so, from this starting-point, to explain the whole mass of different theoretical products and forms of consciousness, religion, philosophy, ethics, etc., etc., and trace their origins and growth, by which means, of course, the whole thing can be shown in its totality (and therefore, too, the reciprocal action of these various sides on one another). It has not, like the idealistic view of history, in every period to look for a category, but remains constantly on the real ground of history; it does not explain practice from the idea but explains the formation of ideas from material practice. . . . Not criticism but revolution is the driving force of history, also of religion, of philosophy and all other types of theory. It shows that history does not end by being resolved into "self-consciousness" as "spirit of the spirit," but that in it at each stage there is found a material result: a sum of productive forces, a historically created relation of individuals to nature and to one another, which is handed down to each generation from its predecessor; a mass of productive forces, different forms of capital, and conditions, which, indeed, is modified by the new generation on the one hand, but also on the other prescribes for it its conditions of life and gives it a definite development, a special character. It shows that circumstances make men just as much as men make circumstances . . .

History is nothing but the succession of the separate generations, each of which exploits the materials, the forms of capital, the productive forces handed down to it by all preceding ones, and thus on the one hand continues the traditional activity in completely changed circumstances and, on the other, modifies the old circumstances with a completely changed activity. This can be speculatively distorted so that later history is made the goal of earlier history, e.g. the goal ascribed to the discovery of America is to further the eruption of the French Revolution. . . . The further the separate spheres, which interact on one another, extend in the course of this development, the more the original isolation of the separate nationalities is destroyed by the developed mode of production and intercourse and the division of labour naturally brought forth by these, the more history becomes world-history. Thus, for instance, if in England a machine is invented, which in India or China deprives countless workers of bread, and overturns the whole form of existence of these empires, this invention becomes a world-historical fact . . . This transformation of history into world-history is not indeed a mere abstract act on the part of the "self-consciousness," the world-spirit, or of any other metaphysical spectre, but a quite material, empirically verifiable act, an act the proof of which every individual furnishes as he comes and goes, eats, drinks and clothes himself.

The ideas of the ruling class are in every epoch the ruling ideas: i.e. the class, which is the ruling material force of society, is at the same time its ruling intellectual force. The class which has the means of material production at its disposal, has control at the same time over the means of mental production, so that thereby, generally speaking, the ideas of those who lack the means of mental production are subject to it. The ruling ideas are nothing more than the ideal expression of the dominant material relationships . . . Thus [the] ideas [of the individuals composing the ruling class] are the ruling ideas of the epoch. For instance, in an age and in a country where royal power, aristocracy and bourgeoisie are contending for mastery and where, therefore, mastery is shared, the doctrine of the separation of powers proves to be the dominant idea and is expressed as an "eternal law" . . .

Each new class which puts itself in the place of one ruling before it, is compelled, merely in order to carry through its aim, to represent its interest as the common interest of all the members of society, put in an ideal form; it will give its ideas the form of universality, and represent them as the only rational, universally valid ones. The class making a revolution appears from the very start, merely because it is opposed to a *class*, not as a class but as the representative of the whole of society; it appears as the whole mass of society confronting the one ruling class. It can do this because, to start with, its interest really is more connected with the common interest of all other non-ruling classes, because under the pressure of conditions its interest has not yet been able to develop as the particular interest of a particular class. Its victory, therefore, benefits also many individuals of the other classes which are not winning a dominant position, but only in so far as it now puts these individuals in a position to raise themselves into the ruling class. When the French bourgeoisie overthrew the power of the aristocracy, it thereby made it possible for many proletarians to raise themselves above the proletariat, but only in so far as they became bourgeois. Every new class, therefore, achieves its hegemony only on a broader basis than that of the class ruling previously, in return for which the opposition of the non-ruling class against the new ruling class later develops all the more sharply and profoundly. Both these things determine the fact that the struggle to be waged against this new ruling class, in its turn, aims at a more decided and radical negation of the previous conditions of society than could all previous classes which sought to rule. [*German Ideology,* 1845–46]

If, therefore, the proletariat should overthrow the political rule of the bourgeoisie, its victory would be only temporary, only an episode in the service of the bourgeois revolution, so long as the material conditions which would render necessary the abolition of the bourgeois mode of production, and consequently the definitive overthrow of the political rule of the bourgeoisie, had not yet been created in the course of historical development. From this point of view, the Reign of Terror in France did no more than to clear away the feudal ruins from French soil by its hammer blows.

The anxious and cautious bourgeoisie would have taken decades to perform this work. The bloody action of the people, therefore, prepared the way. Similarly, the overthrow of the absolute monarchy would have been merely a momentary incident, if the economic conditions for the rule of the bourgeois class had not been developed to the point of ripeness.

Men built for themselves a new world, not out of earthly goods, . . . but out of the historical achievements of their shipwrecked world. In the course of development, they have first to create the material conditions for a new society themselves, and no effort of the mind or the will can save them from this destiny. ["Moralizing Criticism," in *Selected Essays*]

LEOPOLD VON RANKE

History Has No Goal

Leopold von Ranke (1795–1886), was, for some fify years of his long life, associated with the university of Berlin. There, in a school which for years had no rival, he trained generations of historians. His historical revolution consisted in a new and "scientific" standard of criticism of sources, which led to the discrediting of many formerly accepted, and in an insistence on the use of primary sources as evidence. He traveled widely in Europe exploring archives, and pioneered the use of Venetian diplomatic reports, since become one of the basic raw materials of the historical industry. This criticism and scholarship were put to the service of Ranke's attempt to present the past "as it actually happened" (wie es eigentlich gewesen), *without passion or bias.*

Among Ranke's voluminous works, some of the best known are the History of the Latin and Teutonic Nations, 1494–1515 *(1824), which included his famous essay* On the Criticism of Writers of Modern History (Zur Kritik neuerer Geschichtschreiber); History of the Popes *(1834–1836);* History of the Reformation in Germany *(1839–1843); and nine volumes of the unfinished* Universal History, *begun in his eighties.*

The following extract comes from a series of lectures delivered by Ranke in 1854 before Maximilian II, King of Bavaria (1811–1864). The king, deeply interested in history and science, was a pupil and admirer of Ranke. A portion of the published discussion between Ranke and King Max is included.

HOW THE CONCEPT "PROGRESS" MIGHT BE INTERPRETED IN HISTORY

If we wanted to suppose, in common with many philosophers, that all of humanity developed from a given original state toward a positive goal, we could conceive of this in two ways. Either a universally dominant will promoted the development of the human race from one point toward the other; or a trace of the spiritual essence, present in humanity, necessarily propels things toward a definite goal. I would consider these views neither philosophically defensible nor historically demonstrable. We cannot declare this

From Leopold von Ranke, *Ueber die Epochen der neueren Geschichte,* in *Weltgeschichte* (Theil IX. 2. Abth. Ed. A. Dove; Leipzig: Duncker & Humblot, 1888), pp. 2–13. Specially translated for this volume by Moltke S. Gram.

point of view philosophically acceptable because, in the former case, it virtually abolishes human freedom and writes off human beings as tools without a will of their own; and, in the latter case, mankind would either have to be God or nothing at all. Nor are these views historically demonstrable either. For one thing, the largest part of humanity still finds itself in the primitive state, in the point of departure itself. And then we must ask: What is progress? Where is the progress of humanity noticeable? There are elements of the mainstream of historical development which are fixed in the Roman and Germanic peoples; here there is indeed an intellectual force that develops itself from stage to stage. Throughout history an historical force of the human mind is unmistakable. This is a movement, begun in pre-historic times, that continues with a certain constancy. Yet there is, in all of humanity, only one system of peoples taking part in the general historical movement; there are others, however, that are excluded from it. But we cannot, in general, regard even those peoples that are caught up in the historical movement as constantly progressing. If we look, for instance, at Asia, we see that culture arose there and that this part of the world has experienced several cultural epochs. Yet the movement there is generally retrogressive. Thus, the oldest epoch of Asiatic culture was the most productive; the second and third epochs, in which Greek and Roman influence dominated, were no longer as significant; and by the time of the invasion of the barbarians—the Mongols—culture in Asia was completely at an end. Faced with this fact, some have tried to fall back on the hypothesis of geographic progression. Still, I must consider it from the very outset an empty assertion, if one assumes (like, for example, Peter the Great) that culture travels around the globe, coming from the East and returning there again.

In the second place, there is another error to be avoided here: namely, the assumption that the progressive development of the centuries encompasses at the same time all branches of human life and technology. History shows us (to take as an example only one factor) that, in the modern period, art flourished most in the fifteenth and the first part of the sixteenth century. Yet it declined most at the end of the seventeenth and in the first three quarters of the eighteenth century. The situation is paralleled by poetry: here, too, there are only brief periods in which this art is really outstanding; . . . it is indeed not the case that this art improves proportionately with the passage of the centuries.

If we thus exclude a geographic law of development, if we must besides accept, as history teaches us, that nations, whose development does not constantly encompass everything, can be ruined—we will perceive more clearly wherein the constant change of humanity really consists. Change is founded upon the separation and combination of the great intellectual tendencies governing humanity. In these tendencies there is, however, always a certain specific direction which is dominant and causes the others to retreat. Thus, in the second half of the sixteenth century the religious factor was so dominant that literature retreated in the face of it. In the eighteenth century, on the other hand, utilitarianism gained so much ground that art and related activities had to give way to it.

In every epoch of mankind, accordingly, a certain general tendency expresses itself; and progress is due to the fact that in every period a certain movement of the human spirit reveals itself which, emphasizing sometimes one and sometimes another tendency, peculiarly manifests itself in that period.

But if one wants to assume—in opposition to the view expressed here—that in every epoch the life of humanity advances according to some law of proportionality, that every generation completely excels the preceding, that the latest is always the preferable, and that what comes before is only the stepping stone for what comes after—this would be an injustice on the part of the Godhead. A generation so mediated would not have a significance in and for itself, since it would be the stepping stone of the following generation and would not stand in an immediate relation to the divine. But I assert: every epoch is immediate to God and its worth does not reside at all in what emanates from it but rather in its own existence, its own identity. In this way the study of history and, more particularly, of the individual life within history, acquires a very peculiar fascination; for now every epoch must be seen as something having its own special merit and appears to be well worth study.

The historian must accordingly look first at how people at a given time thought and lived; then he will find that, apart from certain immutable, eternal main ideas (for example, morality), every epoch has its special character and its own standard. But even though every epoch has its own justification and value, what emerges from it still cannot be overlooked. The historian must, secondly, perceive the difference between individual epochs in order to observe the inner necessity of the succession. Here some progress is unmistakable. I should not, however, assert that it moves in a straight line but rather like a stream that determines its own course. I conceive the Godhead—if I may risk this remark—since no time lies in front of It, as surveying all historical humanity in its totality and finding all equally valuable. The notion of the education of the human race has, to be sure, some truth in it. But before God all generations of humanity have the same rights; and the historian must also see matters in this light.

An unqualified progress, a quite decisive development, is to be assumed, so far as we can discern, in the area of material interests, where a retrogression can hardly occur without a very great revolution. In morality, however, progress cannot be discerned. Moral ideas can, of course, be spread abroad; and so one can assert also with respect to cultural matters that, for example, the great works which art and literature created are enjoyed these days by a greater number of people than before. It would, however, be laughable to want to be a greater epic writer than Homer or a greater tragedian than Sophocles.

WHAT MIGHT BE THOUGHT OF SO-CALLED DOMINANT IDEAS IN HISTORY

Philosophers—primarily, however, the Hegelian school—have set forth certain ideas about this, according to which the history of humanity spins itself out like a logical process in position, opposition, and mediation, in positive and negative. But life perishes in this scholasticism; and this view of history, this process of the mind developing itself according to various logical categories, would also lead back to what we already rejected above. According to this view, only the Idea would have an independent life, while all mankind would be mere shadows or schemata which realized themselves by means of the Idea. A highly unworthy conception of God and humanity is at the bottom of the doctrine that the World-Spirit brings things about, as it were, through deceit, and exploits human desires to achieve its ends; it can also consistently lead only to Pantheism. Humanity then becomes God in the making, who gives birth to himself through an intellectual process lying in his nature.

Thus, I can understand by dominant ideas nothing other than the ruling tendencies in every century. These tendencies can, of course, be described but not ultimately summed up in a single concept.

Otherwise we would once again come back to what we rejected above.

The historian must sort out the large tendencies of the centuries and present the mainstream of human history, which is just the complex of these various tendencies. I cannot conceive the matter otherwise than that, in the perspective of the divine Idea, mankind has within itself an infinite variety of ways to develop, which gradually make their appearance according to laws, unknown to us, which are more mysterious and greater than one thinks.

DISCUSSION

King Max: You spoke of moral progress. Did you have in mind the inner progress of the individual as well?

Ranke: No, simply the progress of the human race; the individual, on the other hand, must always raise himself to a higher moral level.

King Max: But since humanity is composed of individuals, it is open to question whether, as the individual raises himself to a higher level, this progress will not also include all of humanity.

Ranke: The individual dies; it has a finite existence; humanity itself, an infinite existence. In material matters I assume a progress because one thing evolves out of another; it is otherwise in an ethical context. I believe that in every generation the real moral greatness is the same as that in every other, and that there is no moral greatness to a higher power. We cannot, for example, exceed the moral greatness of antiquity. . . .

King Max: But haven't a greater number of individuals progressed to a higher moral development today than earlier?

Ranke: I concede that, but not as a matter of principle. For history teaches us that many peoples are not even capable of having a culture and that early epochs were often much more moral than were later ones. France in the middle of the seventeenth century, for example, was much more moral and cultured than at the end of the eighteenth century. As I said, a greater diffusion of moral ideas can be asserted, but only in certain areas. Considered from a general human point of view, it seems to me probable that the idea of humanity, historically represented only in the great nations, will gradually encompass all of humanity; and this would then be the inner moral progress. History neither proves nor disproves this view. We must especially guard ourselves against elevating this view to a principle of history. Our task is merely to keep to the facts.

The concept of progress with which our introductory discussion was primarily concerned is, as we saw, not applicable to various things. It is not applicable to the connection of centuries in general; that is, one cannot say that one century is subservient to another. Further, this concept is not applicable to the creations of genius in art, poetry, science, and civic affairs; for all of these are immediately related to the divine. They are, to be sure, temporal; but the act of creation itself is independent of what goes before and what follows. Thus Thucydides, who created historiography, has remained in his own way unsurpassable.

Just as little could we assume a progress in the moral or religious life of the individual; for this, too, has an immediate relation to the Godhead. One could at best concede that earlier concepts of morality were imperfect; but since Christianity has appeared with the true morality and religion, no progress in this regard could take place. It would also be correct to say, for example, that certain national conceptions like the permissibility of revenge, dominant among the Greeks, were purified by Christianity; but what is essential in Christianity was not for that reason prepared by earlier, imperfect conditions. For Christianity is a sudden divine appearance which, like all the great creations of genius, carries within it the character of immediate inspiration. After Plato there can be no other Plato; and little as I minimize Schelling's service to philosophy, I still do not believe that he has outdone Plato. . . .

Progress is, however, to be assumed in everything that relates to the knowledge and control of nature. The former was in its childhood in antiquity; nor can antiquity be compared with us in the latter respect either. This is further connected with what we call expansion. Expansion of moral and religious ideas, of the ideas of humanity in general, ceaselessly progresses; and where once a centre of culture exists, culture has the tendency to expand in all directions—yet not in such a way that we could say that progress is at no point arrested. Hence, in more material matters, in the development and application of the exact sciences, as in the education of the various nations and individuals in the idea of humanity and culture, progress is unqualified.

There is, however, a question in particular humanities, namely philosophy and politics, whether progress has in fact occurred. In philosophy I must confess that the traditional philosophy, as we find it developed in Plato and Aristotle, suffices for me. Formally, we

have never gone beyond it; and more recent philosophers are returning to the substance of Aristotle's position as well. The same is true
of politics: the general principles are stated with certitude in the
ancients, however much richer succeeding periods have grown in
experience and political ventures. Contemporary politics naturally
rests on conditions that are given by history. . . . Later periods
enjoy an advantage over antiquity only in that a greater fullness of
political experience is at their disposal. Likewise, the issue of popular sovereignty cannot be settled by science; it is, instead, to be
settled historically by the grouping of factions. What I have said
about politics applies also to historiography. As I have already mentioned, nobody can pretend to be a greater historian than Thucydides; yet I claim to be accomplishing something in historiography
different from the ancients because our history is richer than theirs,
because we seek to include factors in history which encompass the
entire life of nations, because, in short, we seek to grasp history in
its unity.

JOHN STUART MILL

The Positivist Conception of History

John Stuart Mill (1806–1873), in an astonishing feat of industry and intellectual power, survived the prodigious education which his father James Mill, a disciple and associate of Jeremy Bentham, planned for him. In his Autobiography, Mill himself has given the most balanced account of what he gained and what he lost by it. At least it equipped him, while holding a highly responsible post in the London office of the East India Company, which then ruled British India, to write extensively and influentially on politics, economics, and philosophy. He addressed himself not only to theoretical discussion, but also to immediate issues of the day, and was not afraid to support unpopular causes. Among his many significant works are On Liberty (1859) *and* Utilitarianism (1861).

§ 1. There are two kinds of sociological inquiry. In the first kind, the question proposed is, what effect will follow from a given cause, a certain general condition of social circumstances being presupposed. As, for example, what would be the effect of . . . introducing universal suffrage, in the present condition of society and civilization in any European country . . . But there is also a second inquiry, namely, what are the laws which determine those general circumstances themselves. In this last the question is, not what will be the effect of a given cause in a certain state of society, but what are the causes which produce, and the phenomena which characterize, States of Society generally. In the solution of this question consists the general Science of Society . . .

§ 2. In order to conceive correctly the scope of this general science, and distinguish it from the subordinate departments of sociological speculation, it is necessary to fix the ideas attached to the phrase, "a State of Society." What is called a state of society, is the simultaneous state of all the greater social facts or phenomena. Such are . . . the state of industry, of wealth and its distribution; the habitual occupations of the community; their division into classes, and the relations of those classes to one another; the common beliefs which they entertain; . . . their form of government, and the more important of their laws and customs . . .

From J. S. Mill, *A System of Logic Ratiocinative and Inductive*, 8th ed. (London: Longmans, Green & Co., Ltd., 1961), Bk. VI, Chap. 10 (excerpted).

When states of society, and the causes which produce them, are spoken of as a subject of science, it is implied that there exists a natural correlation among these different elements; that not every variety of combination of these general social facts is possible, but only certain combinations; that, in short, there exist Uniformities of Coexistence between the states of the various social phenomena. And such is the truth . . .

But the uniformities of coexistence obtaining among phenomena which are effects of causes, must (as we have so often observed) be corollaries from the laws of causation by which these phenomena are really determined. The mutual correlation between the different elements of each state of society, is therefore a derivative law, resulting from the laws which regulate the succession between one state of society and another: for the proximate cause of every state of society is the state of society immediately preceding it. The fundamental problem, therefore, of the social science, is to find the laws according to which any state of society produces the state which succeeds it and takes its place . . .

§ 3. . . . One of the thinkers who earliest conceived the succession of historical events as subject to fixed laws, and endeavoured to discover these laws by an analytical survey of history, Vico, the celebrated author of the *Scienza Nuova,* . . . conceived the phenomena of human society as revolving in an orbit; as going through periodically the same series of changes. Though there were not wanting circumstances tending to give some plausibility to this view, it would not bear a close scrutiny: and those who have succeeded Vico in this kind of speculations have universally adopted the idea of a trajectory or progress, in lieu of an orbit or cycle.

The words Progress and Progressiveness, are not here to be understood as synonymous with improvement and tendency to improvement. It is conceivable that the laws of human nature might determine . . . a certain series of changes in man and society, which might not . . . be improvements. It is my belief indeed that the general tendency is, and will continue to be, saving occasional and temporary exceptions, one of improvement; a tendency towards a better and happier state. This, however, is not a question of the method of the social science, but a theorem of the science itself . . .

The progressiveness of the human race is the foundation on which a method of philosophizing in the social science has been of late years erected . . . This method . . . consists in attempting, by a study and analysis of the general facts of history, to discover . . . the law of progress . . . The principal aim of historical speculation in France, of late years, has been to ascertain this law. But while I gladly acknowledge the great services which have been rendered to historical knowledge by this school, I cannot but deem them to be mostly chargeable with a fundamental misconception . . . [It] consists in supposing that the order of succession which we may be able to trace among the different states of society and civilization which history presents to us, . . . could ever amount to a law of nature. It can only be an empirical law. The succession of states of the human mind and of human society cannot have an independent law of its own; it must depend on the psychological and ethological [1] laws which govern the action of circumstances on men and of men on circumstances . . . M. Comte alone, among the new-historical school, has seen the necessity of thus connecting all our generalizations from history with the laws of human nature.

§ 4. But, while it is an imperative rule never to introduce any generalization from history into the social science unless sufficient grounds can be pointed out for it in human nature, I do not think any one will contend that it would have been possible, setting out from the principles of human nature and from the general circumstances of the position of our species, to determine *a priori* the order in which human development must take place . . . So long a series of actions and reactions between Circumstances and Man, each successive term being composed of an ever greater number and variety of parts, could not possibly be computed by human faculties from the elementary laws which produce it . . .

If, therefore, the series of the effects themselves did not, when examined as a whole, manifest any regularity, we should in vain attempt to construct a general science of society . . . But . . . History . . . does, when judiciously examined, afford Empirical Laws of Society. And the problem of general sociology is to ascertain these, and connect them with the laws of human nature, by deduc-

---

[1] Mill gave the name ethology (from the Greek *ethos*, which he translated as "character") to a projected science which was to determine the kind of character produced, in conformity to the general laws of psychology, by any set of circumstances, physical or moral. Sometimes Mill referred to ethology simply as "the science of the formation of character"; and he described it as "the science which corresponds to the art of education." [A *System of Logic*, Bk. VI, Chap. 5, esp. § 4.]—Ed.

tions showing that such were the derivative laws naturally to be expected as the consequences of those ultimate ones.

It is, indeed, hardly ever possible, even after history has suggested the derivative law, to demonstrate *a priori* that such was the only order of succession or of coexistence in which the effects could, consistently with the laws of human nature, have been produced. We can at most make out that there were strong *a priori* reasons for expecting it . . . Often we cannot do even this; we cannot even show that what did take place was probable *a priori*, but only that it was possible. This, however . . . is a real process of verification . . . The empirical laws must be the result of but a few instances, since few nations have ever attained at all, and still fewer by their own independent development, a high stage of social progress. If, therefore, even one or two of these few instances be insufficiently known, or imperfectly analysed into their elements, and therefore not adequately compared with other instances, nothing is more probable than . . . that a wrong empirical law will emerge instead of the right one . . . The only check or corrective is, constant verification by psychological and ethological laws. We may add to this, that no one but a person competently skilled in those laws is capable of preparing the materials for historical generalization . . .

§ 5. The Empirical Laws of Society are of two kinds; some are uniformities of coexistence, some of succession . . . The first branch of the science ascertains the conditions of stability in the social union: the second, the laws of progress. Social Dynamics is the theory of Society considered in a state of progressive movement; while Social Statics is . . . the theory of the mutual actions and reactions of contemporaneous social phenomena . . .

§ 6. . . . In the study of social dynamics . . . the aim is to observe and explain the sequences of social conditions. This branch of the social science would be as complete as it can be made, if every one of the leading general circumstances of each generation were traced to its causes in the generation immediately preceding. But . . . in the filiation of one generation and another, it is the whole which produces the whole, rather than any part a part. Little progress, therefore, can be made in establishing the filiation, directly from laws of human nature, without having first ascertained the immediate or derivative laws according to which social states generate one another as society advances; the *axiomata media* of General Sociology.

The empirical laws which are most readily obtained by generalization from history do not amount to this. They are not the "middle principles" themselves, but only evidence towards the establishment of such principles. They consist of certain general tendencies which may be perceived in society . . . It is easily seen, for instance, . . . that the occupation of all that portion of mankind who are not under external restraint is at first chiefly military, but society becomes progressively more and more engrossed with productive pursuits, and the military spirit gradually gives way to the industrial; to which many similar truths might be added . . .

§ 7. In order to obtain better empirical laws, . . . it is necessary to combine the statical view of social phenomena with the dynamical, considering not only the progressive changes of the different elements, but the contemporaneous condition of each; and thus obtain empirically the law of correspondence not only between the simultaneous states, but between the simultaneous changes, of those elements. This law of correspondence it is, which, duly verified *a priori,* would become the real scientific derivative law of . . . development . . . It would evidently be a great assistance if it should happen to be the fact, that some one element in the complex existence of social man is pre-eminent over all others as the prime agent of the social movement . . .

Now, the evidence of history and that of human nature combine, by a striking instance of consilience, to show that there really is one social element which is thus predominant . . . This is, the state of the speculative faculties of mankind; including the nature of the beliefs which by any means they have arrived at, concerning themselves and the world by which they are surrounded . . . The impelling force to most of the improvements effected in the arts of life, is the desire of increased material comfort; but . . . the state of knowledge at any time is the limit of the industrial improvements possible at that time; and the progress of industry must follow, and depend on, the progress of knowledge . . . Further, as the strongest propensities of uncultivated or half-cultivated human nature . . . tend in themselves to disunite mankind, . . . social existence is only possible by a disciplining of those more powerful propensities, which consists in subordinating them to a common system of opinions . . . But in order that mankind should conform their actions to any set of opinions, these opinions . . . must be believed by them. And thus . . . the character of the propositions assented to by the intellect, essentially determines the moral and political state of the community, as we have already seen that it determines the physical.

These conclusions, deduced from the laws of human nature, are in entire accordance with the general facts of history. Every considerable change historically known to us in the condition of any portion of mankind, when not brought about by external force, has been preceded by a change, of proportional extent, in the state of their knowledge, or in their prevalent beliefs . . .

From this accumulated evidence, we are justified in concluding, that the order of human progression in all respects will mainly depend on the order of progression in the intellectual convictions of mankind . . . The question remains, whether this law can be determined; at first from history as an empirical law, then converted into a scientific theorem by deducing it *a priori* from the principles of human nature . . .

§ 8. The investigation which I have thus endeavoured to characterize, has been systematically attempted, up to the present time, by M. Comte alone . . . I shall confine myself to mentioning one important generalization, which M. Comte regards as the fundamental law of the progress of human knowledge. Speculation he conceives to have, on every subject of human inquiry, three successive stages; in the first of which it tends to explain the phenomena by supernatural agencies, in the second by metaphysical abstractions, and in the third or final state confines itself to ascertaining their laws of succession and similitude. This generalization appears to me to have that high degree of scientific evidence, which is derived from the concurrence of the indications of history with the probabilities derived from the constitution of the human mind. Nor could it be easily conceived, from the mere enunciation of such a proposition, what a flood of light it lets in upon the whole course of history . . .

But whatever decision competent judges may pronounce on the results arrived at by any individual inquirer, the method now characterized is that by which the derivative laws of social order and of social progress must be sought. By its aid we may hereafter succeed . . . in determining what artificial means may be used, and to what extent, to accelerate the natural progress in so far as it is beneficial; . . . and to guard against the dangers or accidents to which our species is exposed from the necessary incidents of its progression. Such practical instructions, founded on the highest branch of speculative sociology, will form the noblest and most beneficial portion of the Political Art.

That of this science and art even the foundations are but beginning to be laid, is sufficiently evident. But the superior minds are fairly turning themselves towards that object. It has become the aim of really scientific thinkers to connect by theories the facts of universal history: it is acknowledged to be one of the requisites of a general system of social doctrine, that it should explain, so far as the data exist, the main facts of history; and a Philosophy of History is generally admitted to be at once the verification, and the initial form, of the Philosophy of the Progress of Society.

KARL POPPER

Historical and Generalizing Sciences

Born and educated in Vienna, Professor Popper (1902–   ) is now Professor of Logic and Scientific Method in the University of London; he has lectured widely in America and Europe. Among his books are The Logic of Scientific Discovery *(1959, first published in German in 1934);* The Open Society and Its Enemies *(1945); and* The Poverty of Historicism *(1957).*

In history no less than in science, we cannot avoid a point of view; and the belief that we can must lead to self-deception and to lack of critical care. This does not mean, of course, that we are permitted to falsify anything, or to take matters of truth lightly. Any particular historical description of facts will be simply true or false, however difficult it may be to decide upon its truth or falsity.

So far, the position of history is analogous to that of the natural sciences, for example, that of physics. But if we compare the part played by a 'point of view' in history with that played by a 'point of view' in physics, then we find a great difference. In physics, as we have seen, the 'point of view' is usually presented by a physical theory which can be tested by searching for new facts. In history, the matter is not quite so simple.

Let us first consider a little more closely the rôle of the theories in a natural science such as physics. Here, theories have several connected tasks. They help to unify science, and they help to explain as well as to predict events. Regarding explanation and prediction, I may perhaps quote from one of my own publications: 'To give a *causal explanation* of a certain event means to derive deductively a statement (it will be called a *prognosis*) which describes that event, using as premises of the deduction some *universal laws* together with certain singular or specific sentences which we may call *initial conditions*. For example, we can say that we have given a causal

From K. R. Popper *The Open Society and Its Enemies* (3d ed.; London: Routledge & Kegan Paul Ltd., 1957), Vol. II, pp. 261–265. Used by permission of Routledge, and of Princeton University Press.

explanation of the breaking of a certain thread if we find that this thread was capable of carrying one pound only, and that a weight of two pounds was put on it. If we analyse this causal explanation, then we find that two different constituents are involved in it. (1) We assume some hypotheses of the character of universal laws of nature; in our case, perhaps: "Whenever a certain thread undergoes a tension exceeding a certain minimum tension which is characteristic for that particular thread, then it will break." (2) We assume some specific statements (the initial conditions) pertaining to the particular event in question; in our case, we may have the two statements: "For this thread, the characteristic minimum tension at which it is liable to break is equal to a one-pound weight" and "The weight put on this thread was a two-pound weight." Thus we have two different kinds of statements which together yield a complete causal explanation, viz.: (1) *universal statements of the character of natural laws,* and (2) *specific statements pertaining to the special case in question, the initial conditions.* . . .

From this analysis of causal explanation, we can see several things. One is that we can never speak of cause and effect in an absolute way, but that an event is a cause of another event, which is its effect, relative to some universal law. However, these universal laws are very often so trivial (as in our own example) that as a rule we take them for granted, instead of making conscious use of them. A second point is that the use of a theory for the purpose of *predicting* some specific event is just another aspect of its use for the purpose of *explaining* such an event. And since we test a theory by comparing the events predicted with those actually observed, our analysis also shows how theories can be *tested.* Whether we use a theory for the purpose of explanation, or prediction, or of testing, depends on our interest, and on what propositions we take as given or assumed.

Thus in the case of the so-called theoretical or *generalizing sciences* (such as physics, biology, sociology, etc.) we are predominantly interested in the universal laws or hypotheses. We wish to know whether they are true, and since we can never directly make sure of their truth, we adopt the method of eliminating the false ones. Our interest in the specific events, for example in experiments which are described by the initial conditions and prognoses, is somewhat limited; we are interested in them mainly as means to certain ends, means by which we can test the universal laws, which latter are considered as interesting in themselves, and as unifying our knowledge.

In the case of applied sciences, our interest is different. The engineer who uses physics in order to build a bridge is predominantly interested in a prognosis: whether or not a ·bridge of a certain kind described (by the initial conditions) will carry a certain load. For him, the universal laws are means to an end and taken for granted.

Accordingly, pure and applied generalizing sciences are respectively interested in testing universal hypotheses, and in predicting specific events. But there is a further interest, that in explaining a specific or particular event. If we wish to explain such an event, for example, a certain road accident, then we usually tacitly assume a host of rather trivial universal laws (such as that a bone breaks under a certain strain, or that any motor-car colliding in a certain way with any human body will exert a strain sufficient to break a bone, etc.), and are interested, predominantly, in the initial conditions or in the cause which, together with these trivial universal laws, would explain the event in question. We then usually assume certain initial conditions hypothetically, and attempt to find some further evidence in order to find out whether or not these hypothetically assumed initial conditions are true; that is to say, we test these specific hypotheses by deriving from them (with the help of some other and usually equally trivial universal laws) new predictions which can be confronted with observable facts.

Very rarely do we find ourselves in the position of having to worry about the universal laws involved in such an explanation. It happens only when we observe some new or strange kind of event, such as an unexpected chemical reaction. If such an event gives rise to the framing and testing of new hypotheses, then it is interesting mainly from the point of view of some generalizing science. But as a rule, if we are interested in specific events and their explanation, we take for granted all the many universal laws which we need.

Now the sciences which have this interest in specific events and in their explanation may, in contradistinction to the generalizing sciences, be called the *historical sciences*.

This view of history makes it clear why so many students of history and its method insist that it is the particular event that interests them, and not any so-called universal historical laws. For from our point of view, there can be no historical laws. Generalization belongs simply to a different line of interest, sharply to be distinguished from that interest in specific events and their causal explanation which is the business of history. Those who are interested in laws must turn to the generalizing sciences (for example, to sociology). Our view also makes it clear why history has so often been described as 'the events of the past as they actually did happen'. This description brings out quite well the specific interest of the student of history, as opposed to a student of a generalizing science, even though we shall have to raise certain objections against it. And our view explains why, in history, we are confronted, much more than in the generalizing sciences, with the problems of its 'infinite subject matter'. For the theories or universal laws of generalizing science introduce unity as well as a 'point of view'; they create, for every generalizing science, its problems, and its centres of interest as well as of research, of logical construction, and of presentation. But in history we have no such unifying theories; or, rather, the host of trivial universal laws we use are taken for granted; they are practically without interest, and totally unable to bring order into the subject matter. If we explain, for example, the first division of Poland in 1772 by pointing out that it could not possibly resist the combined power of Russia, Prussia, and Austria, then we are tacitly using some trivial universal law such as: 'If of two armies which are about equally well armed and led, one has a tremendous superiority in men, then the other never wins.' (Whether we say here 'never' or 'hardly ever' does not make, for our purposes, as much difference as it does for the Captain of H.M.S. *Pinafore.*) Such a law might be described as a law of the sociology of military power; but it is too trivial ever to raise a serious problem for the students of sociology, or to arouse their attention. Or if we explain Caesar's decision to cross the Rubicon by his ambition and energy, say, then we are using some very trivial psychological generalizations which would hardly ever arouse the attention of a psychologist. (As a matter of fact, most historical explanation makes tacit use, not so much of trivial sociological and psychological laws, but of what I have called, in chapter 14, the *logic of the situation;* that is to say, besides the initial conditions describing personal interests, aims, and other situational factors, such as the information available to the person concerned, it tacitly assumes, as a kind of first approximation, the trivial general law that sane persons as a rule act more or less rationally.)

WILHELM DILTHEY

A Non-Positivist Conception of History

Wilhelm Dilthey (1833–1911) crowned a successful academic career by becoming professor of philosophy at Berlin in 1882. He endeavored to provide a "Critique of Historical Reason" for the historical and social studies. His collected works (Gesammelte Schriften, Leipzig, 1914–1936) run to twelve volumes, but little has appeared in English; The Essence of Philosophy, translated by S. A. and S. W. Emery (Chapel Hill, University of North Carolina Press, 1954) and the selections in H. P. Rickman (ed.), Meaning in History. W. Dilthey's Thoughts on History and Society (London, Allen & Unwin, 1961) supplement H. A. Hodges, Wilhelm Dilthey: An Introduction, from which are taken the extracts given below.

THE HISTORICAL BACKGROUND OF DILTHEY'S WORK

At the close of the Middle Age the emancipation of the special sciences began. Yet some of them, the sciences of society and history, remained for a long time, far into the last century, in the old slavery to metaphysics. Worse still, the growing power of the natural sciences involved for them a new relationship of subjection which was not less oppressive than the old. It was the historical school—taking the phrase in a comprehensive sense—which completed the emancipation of the historical consciousness and of historical science. At the very time when, in France, the system of social ideas comprising natural law, natural religion, abstract political theory, and abstract political economy, which had been developed in the seventeenth and eighteenth centuries, was drawing its practical conclusions in the Revolution, and while the armies of this Revolution were besetting and disintegrating the German Empire with its old, curiously ramshackle structure ravaged by the breath of a thousand years of history, there had taken shape in our country a vision of historical growth as the process in which all facts belonging to the mind take their rise, and this vision had revealed the

From H. A. Hodges, *Wilhelm Dilthey: An Introduction* (London: Routledge & Kegan Paul Ltd., 1944), pp. 110–113, 120–124, 137–147. Used by permission of Routledge & Kegan Paul, London.

90

falsity of that entire system of social ideas . . . In the conflicts of European society, whether concerning law, politics, or religion, it made hostile contact everywhere with the ideas of the eighteenth century. In this school there lived a clear empirical eye for facts, a loving penetration into the detail of the historical process, a universal outlook upon history, seeking to determine the value of the particular fact only in terms of the part it plays in development, and a historical spirit in sociology, seeking explanation and guidance for the life of the present day in the study of the past, and in the last resort regarding the life of mind as in every respect a historical product. From this school a stream of new ideas flowed through innumerable channels to all the special sciences.

But hitherto the historical school has not broken through the inner limitations which were bound to hinder its theoretical development and its influence on life. Its study and evaluation of historical phenomena was not brought into relation with the analysis of the facts of consciousness, and so was not based upon what is in the last resort the only secure knowledge; in short, it had no philosophical foundation. It had no healthy relationship with epistemology and psychology. For that reason it also failed to develop an explanatory method: and yet historical contemplation and comparative methods by themselves can neither erect an independent system of the human studies nor obtain influence upon life. So it was that, when Comte, J. S. Mill, and Buckle renewed the attempt to solve the riddle of the historical world by a transference of principles and methods from natural science, the deeper and more vital outlook, which had neither firm foundations nor the power to explicate itself, could make only an ineffective protest against the inferior and more poverty-stricken outlook, which had command of analysis . . .

Thus the need and the plan for an examination of the foundations of the human studies arose spontaneously in my mind. What is the system of principles which underlies alike the historian's judgment, the economist's conclusions, and the jurist's conceptions, and makes it possible to determine their weight? Do its roots reach back into metaphysics? Is there perhaps a philosophy of history or a natural law based on metaphysical conceptions? Or, if that can be dismissed, where can we find a firm support for a system of principles giving connection and certainty to the special studies?

The answers given to these questions by Comte and the positivists, J. S. Mill and the empiricists, seemed to me to mutilate historical reality in order to adapt it to the ideas and methods of the natural sciences. The reaction against this, brilliantly represented by Lotze's *Mikrokosmos*, seemed to me to sacrifice the justified independence of the special sciences, the fruitful power of their empirical methods, and the security of their foundations, in the interests of a sentimental frame of mind, a wistful longing to recall the vanished days when knowledge was a way to the satisfaction of the heart. Nowhere but in inner experience, in the facts of consciousness, did I find a firm anchorage for my thought, and I venture to believe that no reader will be able to escape the force of my argument on this point. All knowledge is knowledge of experience; but the original unity of all experience and its resulting validity are conditioned by the factors which mould the consciousness within which it arises, i.e., by the whole of our nature. This standpoint, which consistently realizes the impossibility of going behind these conditions, of seeing as it were without an eye or directing the gaze of knowledge behind the eye itself, I call the epistemological standpoint; modern knowledge can recognize no other. But then it further became apparent to me that from this standpoint the independence of the human studies finds a foundation such as the historical school required. For from this standpoint our view of the whole natural world turns out to be a mere shadow cast by a reality hidden from us, while it is only in the facts of consciousness given in inner experience that we possess reality as it is.[1] The analysis of these facts lies at the centre of the human studies, and so, in accord with the standpoint of the historical school, in knowing the principles which govern the world of mind we remain within that world, and the human studies form an independent system by themselves. . . .

[1] Elsewhere, Dilthey said: "The datum which is the starting-point of enquiry in the natural sciences is the sensible appearance of bodies of various sizes, which move in space, extend and expand, shrink and diminish, in which changes of character take place. Only by degrees have these sciences made their way to more correct views of the constitution of matter. In this respect our intelligence stands in a much more advantageous relation to the reality of history and society. The unit which is the element in the very complicated structure of society is given immediately to the intelligence—it is itself—while in the natural sciences it has to be inferred. The subjects to which thought, according to its invariable law, attaches the predications through which all knowledge comes about, are in the natural sciences elements which are obtained by a division of external reality, a breaking and splitting up of things, and then only as hypotheses; in the human studies they are real units given as facts in inner experience." [Hodges, *op. cit.*, pp. 144–145.]

UNDERSTANDING AND RELIVING

Understanding has always something individual for its object . . .
The secret of the person invites us of its own accord to ever new
and deeper attempts to understand. And in such understanding
there is opened up the realm of individuals which embraces human
beings and their creations. Herein lies the most characteristic service rendered by understanding to the human studies. Objective
mind [2] and the power of the individual together determine the
world of mind. History rests on the understanding of both. . . .

A lyrical poem enables us by the sequence of its lines to relive a
connected mass of lived experience: not the actual experience which
stimulated the poet, but that which, on the basis of it, the poet puts
into the mouth of an ideal person. The sequence of scenes in a play
enables us to relive segments of the lives of the persons represented. The narrative of the novelist or the historian, which follows
the historical process, produces in us a reliving of that process. It is
the triumph of reliving that, in it, the fragments of a process are so
filled out that we think we have a continuous whole before us . . .

And in this reliving lies an important part of the gain of mental
treasure which we owe to the historian and the poet. The life-
process brings about in every man a continual determination by
which the possibilities inherent in him come to be limited. The crystallization of his nature constantly determines his further development. In short, whether he contemplates the fixity of his circumstances or the form of his acquired experience, he always finds that
the circle of new perspectives upon life and inner changes of his
personal character is a limited one. But understanding opens to him
a wide realm of possibilities which are not to hand in the determina-

---

[2] By "objective mind" Dilthey said, "I understand . . . the manifold forms
in which the common background subsisting among various individuals has
objectified itself in the sensible world. In this objective mind the past is for us
a permanent enduring present. Its realm extends from the style of life and the
forms of economic intercourse to the whole system of ends which society has
formed for itself, to morality, law, the State, religion, art, science and philosophy . . . It is also the medium in which the understanding of other persons and their expressions takes place. . . . Every square planted with trees,
every room in which chairs are arranged, is intelligible to us from our infancy,
because every square and every object in the room has had its place assigned
to it by the common human activities of planning, arranging, and value-deter-
mining." . . . [Hodges, *op. cit.*, p. 118.]

tion of his actual life. For me, as for most people to-day, the possibility of living through religious experiences in my own person is narrowly circumscribed. But when I run through Luther's letters and writings, the accounts given by his contemporaries, the records of the religious conferences and councils and of his official activities, I live through a religious process of such eruptive power, of such energy, in which the stake is life or death, that it lies beyond any possibility of personal experience for a man of our day. But I can relive it . . .

Man, determined from within, can live in imagination through many other existences. Before man limited by circumstances there open out strange beauties in the world, and tracts of life which he can never reach. To generalize—man, bound and determined by the reality of life, is set free not only by art—as has often been shown—but also through the understanding of history. And this effect of history, which its most recent detractors have not seen, is broadened and deepened on the wider levels of the historical consciousness. . . .

THE PECULIAR NATURE OF THE HUMAN STUDIES

We can . . . mark off the human studies from the natural sciences by quite clear criteria. These lie in the attitude of mind . . . by which, in contrast with natural-scientific knowledge, the object of the human studies is constituted. Mankind, if apprehended only by perception and perceptual knowledge, would be for us a physical fact, and as such it would be accessible only to natural-scientific knowledge. It becomes an object for the human studies only in so far as human states are consciously lived, in so far as they find expression in living utterances, and in so far as these expressions are understood. Of course this relationship of life, expression, and understanding embraces not only the gestures, looks, and words in which men communicate, or the enduring mental creations in which the depths of the creator's mind open themselves to the spectator, or the permanent objectifications of mind in social structures, through which the common background of human nature shines and is permanently visible and certain to us. The mind-body unit of life is known to itself through the same double relationship of lived experience and understanding, it is aware of itself in the present, it rediscovers itself in memory as something that once was; but when it tries to hold fast and to apprehend its states, when it turns its attention upon itself, the narrow limits of such an introspective method of self-knowledge make themselves felt. Only from his actions, his fixed utterances, his effects upon others, can man learn about himself; thus he learns to know himself only by the round-about way of understanding. What we once were, how we developed and became what we are, we learn from the way in which we acted, the plans which we once adopted, the way in which we made ourselves felt in our vocation, from old dead letters, from judgments on us which were spoken long ago. In short, it is through the process of understanding that life in its depths is made clear to itself, and on the other hand we understand ourselves and others only when we transfer our own lived experience into every kind of expression of our own and other people's life. Thus everywhere the relation between lived experience, expression, and understanding is the proper procedure by which mankind as an object in the human studies exists for us. The human studies are thus founded on this relation between lived experience, expression, and understanding. Here for the first time we reach a quite clear criterion by which the delimitation of the human studies can be definitively carried out. A study belongs to the human studies only if its object becomes accessible to us through the attitude which is founded on the relation between life, expression, and understanding. . . .

HERMENEUTICS

True, the human studies have an advantage over all knowledge of nature in that their object is not a phenomenon given in sensation, a mere reflection in consciousness of something real, but immediate inner reality itself, and this moreover in the form of a connected system enjoyed from within. Yet the very manner in which this reality is given in *inner experience* gives rise to great difficulties in apprehending it objectively. . . . It is only in comparing myself with others that I come to experience what is individual in myself; only then do I become conscious of that in my own existence which differs from others. . . . The existence of others is in the first instance given to us only from without, in facts of sensation, in gestures, sounds, and actions. It is only by a process of reconstructing that which thus falls under the observation of our senses in particular signs that we add this inner reality. Everything —the content, the structure, the most individual traits of this interpretative addition—has to be transferred from our own life. Now, how can a consciousness with an individual cast of its own attain to objective knowledge of another and a quite differently constituted individuality by means of this kind of reconstruction? . . .

We call the process in which, from signs given outwardly to the senses, we know an inner reality, by the name of *understanding*. . . . We mean . . . by understanding, the process in which from signs given to the senses we come to know a psychic reality whose manifestation they are.

This understanding extends from the apprehension of a child's babble to that of *Hamlet* or the *Critique of Pure Reason*. From stones, marble, musically formed sounds, from gestures, words and writing, from actions, economic institutions and constitutions, the same human mind speaks to us and calls for exegesis. And the process of understanding, so far as it is determined by the common conditions and media of this mode of knowledge, must everywhere have common marks. In these fundamental points it is the same. If I set out to understand, e.g., Leonardo, the interpretation of actions, paintings, pictures and writings works together in a homogeneous unitary process.

Understanding shows various grades. These are conditioned in the first instance by interest. If the interest is limited, so is the understanding. How impatiently we listen to many an explanation! We hold on to one point in it, which is of practical importance to us, without having any interest in the inner life of the speaker. Whereas in other cases we strive keenly to press through every facial expression and every word into the inner mind of a speaker. But even the keenest attention cannot become a skilled process, in which a controllable degree of objectivity is reached, unless the manifestation of life is fixed so that we can return to it again and again. Such *skilled understanding of permanently fixed manifestations of life we call exegesis or interpretation*. . . .

This art of interpretation has developed just as gradually, regularly, and slowly as, e.g., the art of questioning nature by experiment. It arose and maintains itself in the personal mastery of the able philologist. Hence too it is naturally handed on to others predominantly through personal contact with the great master of exegesis or with his work. But at the same time every art proceeds according to *rules*. These teach us how to overcome difficulties. They hand on the gains acquired by personal skill. Hence out of the art of exegesis there early took shape the *exposition* of its *rules*. And out of the conflict between these rules, out of the struggle between various tendencies over the exegesis of vitally important works and the consequent need to find a basis for the rules, arose the science of hermeneutics. It is the *technique* of the *exegesis* of *written records*.

R. G. COLLINGWOOD

Scientific History: Its Methods and Presuppositions

[THE SCIENTIFIC REVOLUTION IN HISTORIOGRAPHY]

The chief business of twentieth-century philosophy is to reckon with twentieth-century history. Until the late nineteenth and early twentieth centuries, historical studies had been in a condition analogous to that of natural science before Galileo.[1] In Galileo's time something happened to natural science (only a very ignorant or a very learned man would undertake to say briefly what it was) which suddenly and enormously increased the velocity of its progress and the width of its outlook. About the end of the nineteenth century something of the same kind was happening, more gradually and less spectacularly perhaps, but not less certainly, to history.

Until then, the writer of history had been in the last resort, however he might prune and pad, moralize and comment, a scissors-and-paste man. At bottom, his business was to know what 'the authorities' had said about the subject he was interested in, and to his authorities' statements he was tied by the leg, however long the rope and however flowery the turf over which it allowed him to circle. If his interest led him towards a subject on which there were no authorities, it led him into a desert where nothing was except the sands of ignorance and the mirage of imagination.

I will not pretend that my first visit to a modern excavation (it was my father's dig at the north tower of the Roman fort

From R. G. Collingwood, *An Autobiography* (London: Oxford University Press, 1939), pp. 79–81, 108–112, 127–135. Used by permission of the Clarendon Press, Oxford.

[1] Lord Acton in his Cambridge inaugural lecture in 1895 said very truly that historical studies had entered upon a new era in the second quarter of the nineteenth century. It would be an understatement to say that since 1800 history has passed through a Copernican revolution. Looking back from the present day one sees that a much greater revolution has been accomplished than that associated with the name of Copernicus.

called Hardknot Castle; I was three weeks old, and they took me in a carpenter's bag) opened my eyes to the possibility of something different. But I grew up in a gradually thickening archaeological atmosphere; for my father, who as a professional painter was not very successful, turned more and more as he grew older to archaeology, for which he was brilliantly gifted; and at last, during school holidays, I learnt to distinguish the relics of ancient camps and cultivations from eskers and outcrops, was entrusted with the search for prehistoric remains in unexplored districts and the surveying of them when found, and spent two seasons working as his assistant in his now classical excavation of a Romano-British village.

This and similar experiences taught me that scissors and paste were not the only foundation of historical method. All you wanted, I could see, was a sufficiently extensive and sufficiently scientific development of such work, and it would teach you, not indeed everything, but a great deal, about subjects whose very existence must remain permanently unknown to historians who believed in authorities. I could see, too, that the same methods might be used to correct the authorities themselves, where they had been mistaken or untruthful. In either case, the idea of an historian as depending on what the authorities tell him was exploded. . . .

[HOW HISTORIOGRAPHY DIFFERS FROM THE STUDY OF THE PAST IN NATURAL SCIENCE]

If an archaeologist finds a stratum of earth and stones and mortar, mixed with potsherds and coins, on the top of which is a layer of level flags, supporting more earth with potsherds and coins of a rather different type, it is easy to say that he uses these two sets of potsherds and coins exactly as a geologist uses fossils, to show that the strata belong to different periods and to date them by correlating them with strata found elsewhere and containing relics of the same type.

Easy, but untrue. For the archaeologist, these things are not stone and clay and metal, they are building-stone and potsherds and coins; debris of a building, fragments of domestic utensils, and means of exchange, all belonging to a bygone age whose purposes they reveal to him. He can use them as historical evidence only so far as he understands what each one of them was for. If in the case of one object he does not understand that, he has, as an

archaeologist, no use for the object; he would throw it away,
but that he hopes some one more learned or more resourceful
than himself may solve the riddle. It is not only the minutiae, like
pins and buttons, that he regards as expressions of purpose; he
thinks of the whole building, the whole settlement, in the same
way.

Before the nineteenth century, a natural scientist might have
replied that the same was true of his own studies: was not every
task in natural science a contribution to the decipherment of the
purposes of that mighty being whom some called Nature and
others God? The nineteenth-century scientist would answer quite
firmly that it was not. And the nineteenth-century scientist is right
as to the facts. Natural science as it exists to-day, and has existed
for the best part of a century, does not include the idea of purpose
among its working categories. Perhaps he is right in his theology
too. I cannot think it pious to make our study of Nature depend
on the assumption that the purposes of God are within our grasp;
and if a palaeontologist told me that he never bothered to ask
what trilobites were for, I should be glad, for the sake of his
immortal soul as well as the progress of his science. If archaeology
and palaeontology worked according to the same principles,
trilobites would be as valueless to that palaeontologist as are to
the archaeologist those 'iron implements of uncertain use' which
cause him so much embarrassment.

History and pseudo-history alike consisted of narratives: but in
history they were narratives of purposive activity, and the evidence
for them consisted of relics they had left behind (books or potsherds, the principle was the same) which became evidence precisely
to the extent to which the historian conceived them in terms of
purpose, that is, understood what they were for; in pseudo-history
there is no conception of purpose. . . .

[THE CONDITIONS ON WHICH PAST
THOUGHTS CAN BE KNOWN
HISTORIOGRAPHICALLY]

On what conditions was it possible to know the history of a
thought? First, the thought must be expressed: either in what we
call language, or in one of the many other forms of expressive
activity. Historical painters seem to regard an outstretched arm
and a pointing hand as the characteristic gesture expressing the

thought of a commanding officer. Running away expresses the thought that all hope of victory is gone. Secondly, the historian must be able to think over again for himself the thought whose expression he is trying to interpret. If tor any reason he is such a kind of man that he cannot do this, he had better leave that problem alone. The important point here is that the historian of a certain thought must think for himself that very same thought, not another like it. If some one, hereinafter called the mathematician, has written that twice two is four, and if some one else, hereinafter called the historian, wants to know what he was thinking when he made those marks on paper, the historian will never be able to answer this question unless he is mathematician enough to think exactly what the mathematician thought, and expressed by writing that twice two are four. When he interprets the marks on paper, and says, 'by these marks the mathematician meant that twice two are four', he is thinking simultaneously: (*a*) that twice two are four, (*b*) that the mathematician thought this, too; and (*c*) that he expressed this thought by making these marks on paper. I will not offer to help a reader who replies, 'ah, you are making it easy for yourself by taking an example where history really is the history of thought; you couldn't explain the history of a battle or a political campaign in that way.' I could, and so could you, Reader, if you tried.

This gave me [the] proposition: 'historical knowledge is the re-enactment in the historian's mind of the thought whose history he is studying.' . . .

[HISTORIOGRAPHY AS "BACONIAN"]

If historical studies were to pass through a Baconian revolution— the revolution which converts a blind and random study into one where definite questions are asked and definite answers insisted upon—the first thing to be done was to preach that revolution among the historians themselves. When I began to study Roman Britain the revolution had made a little progress, but not much. Haverfield and his colleagues of the Cumberland Excavation Committee in the eighteen-nineties had been consciously and completely Baconian in their methods. They never dug a trench without knowing exactly what information they were looking for; they knew both that this information was the next thing they needed for the progress of their study, and also that this trench would give it them. That is why they could settle highly intricate and abstruse problems at a cost of never more, and often much less, than thirty or fourty pounds a year. . . .

[HISTORIANS' HYPOTHESES ARE ABOUT INTENTIONS AND PURPOSES: AN EXAMPLE FROM ARCHAEOLOGY]

[One] principle was that, since history proper is the history of thought, there are no mere 'events' in history: what is miscalled an 'event' is really an action, and expresses some thought (intention, purpose) of its agent; the historian's business is therefore to identify this thought.

For the archaeologist this means that all objects must be interpreted in terms of purposes. Whenever you find any object you must ask, 'What was it for?' and, arising out of that question, 'Was it good or bad for it? i.e. was the purpose embodied in it successfully embodied in it, or unsuccessfully?' These questions, being historical questions, must be answered not by guesswork but on historical evidence; any one who answers them must be able to show that his answer is the answer which the evidence demands.

This was the tritest of commonplaces. But the attempt to put it consistently into practice led to some interesting results. For example, the many archaeologists who had worked at the Roman Wall between Tyne and Solway had never, I found, seriously asked themselves what it was for. Vaguely, you could of course call it a frontier defence, and say that it was to keep out the tribes beyond it. But that will no more satisfy the historian than it will satisfy an engineer if you tell him that a marine engine is to drive a ship. How did it work? Was it meant to work, for example, like a town-wall, from the top of which defenders repelled attacks? Several obvious features about it made it quite impossible that any Roman soldier should ever have meant to use it in that way. No one seemed to have noticed this before; but when I pointed it out in 1921 [2] every one who was interested in the subject admitted that it was so, and my counter-suggestion that the wall was meant for an 'elevated sentry-walk' was generally accepted.

A question answered causes another question to arise. If the Wall was a sentry-walk, elevated from the ground and provided

[2] 'The Purpose of the Roman Wall', in *The Vasculum*, vol. viii, no. 1 (Newcastle-upon-Tyne), pp. 4–9.

(no doubt) with a parapet to protect the sentries against sniping, the same sentry-walk must have continued down the Cumberland coast, beyond Bowness-on-Solway, in order to keep watch on vessels moving in the estuary; for it would have been very easy for raiders to sail across and land at any unguarded point between Bowness and St. Bee's Head. But here the sentry-walk need not be elevated, for sniping was not to be feared. There ought, therefore, to be a chain of towers, not connected by a wall but otherwise resembling those on the Wall, stretching down that coast. The question was, did such towers exist?

Search in old archaeological publications showed that towers of exactly the right kind had been found; but their existence had been forgotten, as generally happens with things whose purpose is not understood. Search on the ground in 1928 revealed a number of other places where it seemed possible that others might yet be revealed by future excavation.[3] . . .

[A FURTHER EXAMPLE FROM THE USE OF WRITTEN RECORDS]

The principle applies not merely to archaeology, but to every kind of history. Where written sources are used, it implies that any action attributed by the sources to any character must be understood in the same way. Julius Caesar, we are told, invaded Britain in two successive years. What did he do it for? The question is hardly ever asked by historians; and I can remember none who has tried to answer it scientifically, that is, by means of evidence. There is, of course, no evidence to speak of except that contained in Julius Caesar's own narrative. There he never says what he meant to effect by his invasions of Britain. It is the fact of his silence that constitutes our chief evidence as to what his intention was. Whatever he meant to bring about, his intention was one which he decided to conceal from his readers. In the light of a general acquaintance with the *Commentaries,* the likeliest explanation for this concealment was that whatever his purpose had been he had failed to achieve it. I then compared the strength of his expeditionary force with that of the army sent over by Claudius, nearly a century later, and this settled it. Caesar must have intended no mere punitive expedition or demonstration of force, like that of

[3] 'Roman Signal-stations on the Cumberland Coast', in *Cumb. and West. Antiq. Soc. Trans.* xxix (1929), 138–65.

his German expedition in 55, but the complete conquest of the country . . . This view of mine may be mistaken; but future historians will have to reckon with the question I have raised, and either accept my answer or produce a better one.

People who do not understand historical thinking, but are obsessed by scissors and paste, will say: 'It is useless to raise the question, because if your only information comes from Caesar, and Caesar has not told you his plans, you cannot ever know what they were.' These are the people who, if they met you one Saturday afternoon with a fishing-rod, creel, and camp-stool, walking towards the river, would ask: 'Going fishing?' . . .

[BACONIAN HISTORIOGRAPHY VS. SCISSORS-AND-PASTE]

In describing these researches into historical method, I am taking most of my examples from archaeology (that is, history in which the sources used are 'unwritten' sources, or, more accurately, are not pre-existing narratives of the events into which the historian is inquiring). But this is not because my results did not equally apply to history whose sources are 'written'. The reason I am talking so much about archaeology is that in archaeology the issue raised by the project of a Baconian revolution is unmistakable. When history is based on literary sources the difference between scissors-and-paste or pre-Baconian history, where the historian merely repeats what his 'authorities' tell him, and scientific or Baconian history, where he forces his 'authorities' to answer the questions he puts to them, is not always quite clear. It becomes clear enough on occasion; for example, when he tries to get out of his 'authorities' the answer to a question which they did not expect a reader to ask (as when we try to get out of an ancient writer answers to economic and demographic questions), or when he tries to get out of them facts which they wished to conceal. On other occasions it sometimes does not leap to the eye. In archaeology, however, it is obvious. Unless the archaeologist is content merely to describe what he or some one else has found, which it is almost impossible to do without using some interpretative terms implying purpose, like 'wall', 'pottery', 'implement', 'hearth', he is practising Baconian history all the time: asking about everything he handles, 'What was this for?' and trying to see how it fitted into the context of a peculiar kind of life.

For this reason archaeology has provided a wonderfully sensitive method for answering questions to which not only do literary sources give no direct answer, but which cannot be answered even by the most ingenious interpretation of them.

W. H. DRAY AND C. G. HEMPEL

Historical Explanation:
A Contemporary Controversy

'William H. Dray (1921–   ) was born in Montreal and educated at
Toronto and Oxford. He is now Associate Professor of Philosophy at the
University of Toronto. He is the author of Laws and Explanation in
History (1957).
Carl G. Hempel (1905–   ) was educated in Germany and Vienna.
He left Germany in 1934, and now teaches at Princeton University. He
has published numerous articles in philosophical journals; his writings in
the philosophy of history include the now classic article, "The Function
of General Laws in History" (Journal of Philosophy, XXXIX, 1942), and
"Rational Action" (Proceedings of the American Philosophical Associa-
tion, XXXV, 1962).

I. 'RATIONAL' EXPLANATION IN
HISTORIOGRAPHY, BY W. H. DRAY

Let me try to sketch briefly what I take to be the conceptual foundation of most explanations of human actions in history. The function of
an explanation is to resolve puzzlement of some kind. When an
historian sets out to explain an historical action, his problem
is usually that he does not know what reason the agent had for
doing it. To achieve understanding, what he seeks is information
about what the agent believed to be the facts of his situation,
including the likely results of taking various courses of action considered open to him, and what he wanted to accomplish: his purposes, goals, or motives. Understanding is achieved when the
historian can see the reasonableness of a man's doing what this
agent did, given the beliefs and purposes referred to; his action can
then be explained as having been an "appropriate" one. The point
I want to emphasize is that what is brought out by such considera-
tions is a conceptual connection between understanding a man's

From Philosophy and History: A Symposium, ed. Sidney Hook (New York:
New York University Press, 1963), pp. 108–110, 143–159. Professor Dray's
essay is entitled, "The Historical Explanation of Actions Reconsidered," and
Professor Hempel's is entitled "Reasons and Covering Laws in Historical Explanation." Used by permission of New York University Press.

action and discerning its rationale. As Professor Hook once put it, there is a difference between showing an action to be peculiar and showing it to be confused. There is similarly a difference between showing an action to be routine and showing it to have point.

Explanation which tries to establish a connection between beliefs, motives, and actions of the indicated sort I shall call "rational explanation." The following is a particularly clear example of it. (I hope I may therefore be pardoned for using an example I have used before for the same purpose.)

In trying to account for the success of the invasion of England by William of Orange, Trevelyan asks himself why Louis XIV withdrew military pressure from Holland in the summer of 1688—this action being, he tells us, "the greatest mistake of his life." His answer is: "Louis calculated that, even if William landed in England there would be a civil war and long troubles, as always in that factious island. Meantime he could conquer Europe at leisure." Furthermore, "he was glad to have the Dutch out of the way (in England) while he dealt a blow at the Emperor Leopold (in Germany)." He thought "it was impossible that the conflict between James and William should not yield him an opportunity." What makes Louis' action understandable here, according to Trevelyan, is our discovery of a "calculation" which was "not as absurd as it looks after the event." Indeed, the calculation shows us just how appropriate Louis' unfortunate action really was to the circumstances regarded as providing reasons for it. In fact, of course, the king, in a sense, miscalculated; and his action was, in a sense, not appropriate to the circumstances. Yet the whole purpose of Trevelyan's explanatory account is to show us that, for a man in Louis' position, with the aims and beliefs he had, the action was appropriate at least to the circumstances as they were envisaged.

For explanations of the kind just illustrated, I should argue, the establishment of a deductive logical connection between *explanans* and *explanandum,* based on the inclusion of suitable empirical laws in the former, is neither a necessary nor a sufficient condition of explaining. It is not necessary because the aim of such explanations is not to show that the agent was the sort of man who does in fact always do the sort of thing he did in the sort of circumstances he thought he was in. What it aims to show is that the sort of thing he did made perfectly good sense from his own point of view. The establishment of such a connection, if it could be done, would not be a sufficient condition of such explanation either, since it would not itself represent the relation between the agent's beliefs and purposes and what he did as making the latter a reasonable thing to have done.

I might perhaps add—to avoid possible misunderstanding—that the issue between the appropriateness of applying the covering law and rational "models" to such cases has nothing to do with the question whether historical explanations are to be given in terms of people's "ideas" or in terms of "objective" conditions of their natural and social environment. For Professor Hempel, unlike certain materialist philosophers of history, would allow that the explanation of action is peculiar, at least in the sense of usually and properly making reference to the motives and beliefs of the agents concerned. He would admit, I think, that in offering explanations of the *doing* of actions, by contrast with, say, their success or failure, it is not *actual*, but *envisaged*, states of affairs to which we need to refer. Apart from this, however, explanations of action are, for Hempel, "not essentially different from the causal explanations of physics and chemistry." For "the determining motives and beliefs," he says, ". . . have to be classified among the antecedent conditions of a motivational explanation, and there is no formal difference on this account between motivational and causal explanation." In view of what has been said about non-deducibility of the *explanandum*, it should be clear that my quarrel with this is that it does get the form, not the content, of rational explanations wrong.

II. RATIONAL VS. 'DISPOSITIONAL' EXPLANATION, BY C. G. HEMPEL

DEDUCTIVE AND PROBABILISTIC
EXPLANATION BY COVERING LAWS

The suggestive term 'covering law model of explanation' was introduced by Professor Dray in his monograph, *Laws and Explanation in History*, in which, after a very fair-minded presentation of this conception of explanation, he develops a number of interesting arguments against its general adequacy, particularly in the field of historical inquiry.

In his book, Mr. Dray used the term 'covering law model' to

refer to the construal of an explanation as a deductive subsumption under covering laws. In an explanation of this kind, a given empirical phenomenon—in this paper, I will normally take it to be a particular event—is accounted for by deducing the *explanandum* statement, which describes the event in question, from a set of other statements, called the *explanans*. This set consists of some general laws and of statements describing certain particular facts or conditions, which usually are antecedent to or simultaneous with the event to be explained. In a causal explanation, for example—to mention one important variety of deductive explanation by covering laws—an individual event (e.g., an increase in the volume of a particular body of gas at a particular place and time) is presented as the "effect" of certain other particular events and conditions (e.g., heating of that body of gas under conditions of constant pressure), from which it resulted (from whose realization its occurrence can be inferred) in accordance with certain general laws (e.g., gas laws).

In explanations of the deductive, or "deductive-nomological," kind the covering laws are all of strictly universal form; i.e., schematically speaking, they are statements to the effect that in *all* cases where a certain complex F of conditions is satisfied, an event or state of kind G will come about; in symbolic notation: $(x) (Fx \supset Gx)$.

But there is a second, logically quite different, kind of explanation, which plays an important role in various branches of empirical science, and which I will call "covering law explanation" as well. The distinctive feature of this second type, to which Mr. Dray briefly alludes in his paper, is that some of the covering laws are of probabilistic-statistical form. In the simplest case, a law of this form is a statement to the effect that under conditions of a more or less complex kind F, an event or "result" of kind G will occur with statistical probability—i.e., roughly: with long-run relative frequency—q; in symbolic notation: $p_s(G,F) = q$. If the probability q is close to 1, a law of this type may be invoked to explain the occurrence of G in a given particular case in which conditions F are realized.

By way of a simple illustration, suppose that after one particular rolling of a given set of four dice, the total number of dots facing up is greater than 4. This might be explained by the following information (whose factual correctness is, of course, an empirical matter and subject to empirical test; it would not be true, for example, if one of the dice were loaded): (i) For every one of the dice, the statistical probability for any particular face to show up as a result of a rolling is the same as for any other face, and (ii) the results yielded by the individual dice, when rolled jointly, are statistically independent of each other; so that the statistical probability for a joint rolling (R) of all four dice to yield a total of more than four dots (M) is: $p_s(M,R) = 1295/1296 = .9992$. . . . This general probability statement, combined with the information that the particular occurrence under consideration, say i, was a case of joint rolling of the four dice (or briefly that Ri), does not logically imply that in the particular case i the total number of eyes facing up will be more than four (or that Mi, for short): but the two statements provide strong inductive grounds, or strong inductive support, or, as it is sometimes put, high inductive probability, for the assumption or expectation that Mi. The logical character of this explanatory argument may be represented by the following schema:

(*Explanans*) $\begin{cases} p_s(M,R) = 1295/1296 \\ Ri \end{cases}$ confers high inductive proba-bility on

(*Explanandum*)   Mi

The probability which the *explanans* is here said to confer upon the *explanandum* is clearly not of the statistical kind; it does not represent an empirically determined quantitative relation between two kinds of event, such as R and M; rather, it is a logical relation between two statements—in our case, between the conjunction of the *explanans* statement on one hand and the *explanandum* state-ment on the other . . . In an explanation by means of probabilistic-statistical laws, the "subsumption" of the *explanandum* statement under the "covering laws" rests, not on a deductive implication, but on a relation of inductive support between the *explanans* and the *explanandum* statement. I will therefore refer to this kind of ex-planation as *probabilistic* or *inductive explanation*. . . .

EXPLAINING ACTIONS BY REASONS
Dray holds that the method, widely used by historians among others, of explaining human actions in terms of underlying reasons

cannot be construed as conforming to the covering law pattern: to do so, he says, would be to give the wrong kind of reconstruction, it would get the form of such explanations wrong. In my opinion, Dray's arguments in support of this verdict, and his own alternative construal of such explanations, form a substantial contribution toward the formulation and clarification of the perplexing issues here at stake.

According to Dray, the object of explaining an action by reference to the reasons for which it was done is "to show that what was done was the thing to have done for the reasons given, rather than merely the thing that is done on such occasions, perhaps in accordance with certain laws." The explanatory reasons will include the objectives the agent sought to attain and his beliefs concerning relevant empirical matters, such as the alternative courses of action open to him and their likely consequences. The explanation, according to Dray, then provides "a reconstruction of the agent's *calculation* of means to be adopted toward his chosen end in the light of the circumstances in which he found himself," and it shows that the agent's choice was appropriate, that it was the thing to do under the circumstances. The appraisal thus made of the appropriateness of what was done presupposes, not general laws, but instead what Dray calls a "principle of action," i.e., a normative or evaluative principle of the form 'When in a situation of type C, the thing to do is X.' . . .

Dray's very suggestively presented construal of explanations by reasons has a basic logical defect, which springs from the view that such explanations must be based on principles of action rather than on general laws. Dray explicitly makes a distinction between the two on the ground that the phrase 'the thing to do,' which characteristically occurs in a principle of action, "functions as a value-term," and that therefore there is a certain "element of *appraisal*" in a rational explanation, for it must tell us in what way an action "was *appropriate*." But—and this seems to me the crux of the matter—to show that an action was the appropriate or rational thing to have done under the circumstances is not to explain why in fact it was done. Indeed, no normative or evaluative principle specifying what kind of action is appropriate in given circumstances can possibly serve to explain why a person acted in a particular way; and this is so no matter whether the action does or does not conform to the normative principle in question. . . .

And it seems clear to me that a historian would simply see no point in displaying the appropriateness or rationality of an action if he did not assume that the agent, at the time in question, was disposed to act rationally (as he might not be under conditions of extreme fatigue, under severe emotional strain, under the influence of drugs, and the like). And since, in an explanation by reasons, this essential presupposition will normally be taken for granted, it will not, as a rule, be explicitly mentioned; it is rather when departures from rationality are considered that the need is felt explicitly to specify disturbing circumstances. But while an elliptic formulation that forgoes explicit mention of the assumption of rationality may be quite satisfactory for practical purposes, i.e., in the pragmatic-psychological context of explanation, it obscures the logic of the explanatory argument; and surely, an analysis that makes explicit this essential assumption underlying the historian's account does not thereby force the method of explanation by reasons upon a Procrustean bed.

I think the broadly dispositional analysis I have outlined applies also to the intriguing case, invoked by Mr. Dray, of explaining one's own actions by reference to the reasons for which they were done. To be sure, in an account of the form 'I did X for reasons R,' explanation and justification are almost inextricably fused, and yet, we do distinguish between a genuine explanation and a mere rationalization in such contexts; and an account of the form 'I did X for reasons R' would be suspected of being a rationalization if there were grounds to believe that I had not actually done X for the reasons given: e.g., that I had not in fact had the reasons and beliefs adduced in my account, or that I had been in a state in which I might well have tended not to take an action appropriate to my objectives and relevant empirical beliefs. Thus again, a statement given by me of the reasons for my action can have explanatory force only on the assumption of a disposition to act rationally in the given situation.

Bibliography

GENERAL REFERENCES

Collingwood, R. G. *The Idea of History.* New York: Oxford Univ. Press Galaxy, 1956.

Gardiner, P. (ed.), *Theories of History.* Glencoe, Ill.: The Free Press, 1959. [This also contains a helpful bibliography.]

Gooch, G. P. *History and Historians in the Nineteenth Century.* 2d ed. London: Longmans, 1952.

Theory and Practice in Historical Study: A Report of the Committee on Historiography, Bulletin 54 (1946). New York: Social Science Research Council, 1946.

Walsh, W. H. *Philosophy of History: An Introduction.* Rev. ed. New York: Harper Torchbooks, 1960.

HISTORIANS ON HISTORY

Acton, Lord. "Inaugural Lecture on the Study of History," in *Lectures on Modern History.* New York: Meridian, 1961.

Bloch, M. *The Historian's Craft.* New York: Knopf, 1953.

Namier, L. B. "History," in *Avenues of History.* London: Hamilton, 1952.

CHRISTIANITY AND HISTORY

SAINT AUGUSTINE

Cochrane, C. N. *Christianity and Classical Culture: A Study of Thought and Action from Augustus to Augustine.* London: Oxford Univ. Press, 1944.

Marrou, H. *St. Augustine and His Influence through the Ages,* trans. P. Hepburne-Scott. New York: Harper Torchbooks, 1957.

Mommsen, T. E. "St. Augustine and the Christian Idea of Progress: The Background of *The City of God,*" *Journal of the History of Ideas,* XII (1951).

Portalié, E. *A Guide to the Thought of Saint Augustine,* trans. R. J. Bastian. Chicago: Regnery, 1960.

MODERN CHRISTIANS AND HISTORY

Berdyaev, N. *The Meaning of History,* trans. G. Reavey. New York: Meridian, 1962.

Bultmann, R. *History and Eschatology.* New York: Harper Torchbooks, 1962.

Löwith, K. *Meaning in History: The Theological Implications of the Philosophy of History.* Chicago: Univ. of Chicago Press, 1949.

Maritain, J. *On the Philosophy of History,* ed. J. W. Evans. New York: Scribner's, 1957.

Niebuhr, R. *Faith and History. A Comparison of Christian and Modern Views of History.* New York: Scribner's, 1951.
Tillich, P. *The Interpretation of History,* trans. N. A. Rasetzki and E. L. Talmey. New York: Scribner's, 1936.

VICO

Caponigri, A. R. *Time and Idea: The Theory of History in Giambattista Vico.* London: Routledge, 1953.
Copleston, F. *A History of Philosophy.* London: Burns, 1960. Vol. VI, Chap. 8.
Croce, B. *The Philosophy of Giambattista Vico,* trans. R. G. Collingwood. New York: Macmillan, 1913.

HEGEL AND MARX

Findlay, J. N. *Hegel. A Re-Examination.* London: Allen & Unwin, 1958.
Lichtheim, G. *Marxism. An Historical and Critical Study.* New York: Praeger, 1961.
Marcuse, H. *Reason and Revolution. Hegel and the Rise of Social Theory.* 2d ed. London: Routledge, 1955.
Plamenatz, J. *Man and Society.* London: Longmans, 1963. Vol. II.
Tucker, R. C. *Philosophy and Myth in Karl Marx.* Cambridge: Cambridge Univ. Press, 1961. [And cf. the review essay by the Polish Marxist A. Schaff, *History and Theory,* 1962, II, pp. 307–318.]

RANKE AND THE GROWTH OF SCIENTIFIC HISTORY

RANKE

Acton, Lord, "German Schools of History," *English Historical Review,* I (1886; reprinted in Acton, *Historical Essays and Studies,* ed. J. N. Figgis and R. V. Laurence, London: Macmillan, 1908).
Geyl, P. *Debates with Historians.* New York: Meridian, 1958.
Iggers, G. G. "The Image of Ranke in American and German Historical Thought," *History and Theory,* II (1962).

SCIENTIFIC HISTORY

Berlin, I. "History and Theory: The Concept of Scientific History", *History and Theory,* I (1960).
Engel-Janosi, F. "The Growth of German Historicism," *The Johns Hopkins University Studies in Historical and Political Science.* (Baltimore: Johns Hopkins, 1944). Vol. LXII.
Lee, D. E., and R. N. Beck. "The Meaning of 'Historicism'," *American Historical Review,* LIX (1954).
Meinecke, F. *Machiavellism: The Doctrine of Raison d'Etat and Its Place*

Bibliography / 115

in Modern History, trans. D. Scott. New Haven: Yale Univ. Press, 1957.
Ritter, G. "Scientific History, Contemporary History, and Political Science," *History and Theory*, I (1961).

MILL
Anschutz, R. P. *The Philosophy of J. S. Mill.* Oxford: Clarendon, 1953.
Packe, M. St. J. *The Life of John Stuart Mill.* New York: Macmillan, 1954.
Passmore, J. *A Hundred Years of Philosophy.* London: Duckworth, 1957.

PROGRESS
Burckhardt, J. "On Fortune and Misfortune in History," in *Force and Freedom*, ed. J. H. Nichols. New York: Meridian, 1955.
Bury, J. B. *The Idea of Progress.* New York: Dover, 1955.
Ginsberg, M. *The Idea of Progress. A Revaluation.* Boston: Beacon, 1953.
Kant, I. "An Old Question Raised Again: Is the Human Race Constantly Progressing?" In *Kant on History*, ed. L. W. Beck. Indianapolis: Liberal Arts Press, 1963.

DILTHEY AND COLLINGWOOD
Abel, T. "The Operation Called *Verstehen*," *American Journal of Sociology*, LIV (1948–1949).
Donagan, A. *The Later Philosophy of R. G. Collingwood.* Oxford: Clarendon, 1962.
Hodges, H. A. *The Philosophy of Wilhelm Dilthey.* London: Routledge, 1952.
Walsh, W. H. "R. G. Collingwood's Philosophy of History," *Philosophy*, XXII (1947).

HISTORICAL EXPLANATION
Dray, W. *Laws and Explanation in History.* London: Oxford Univ. Press, 1957.
Gardiner, P. *The Nature of Historical Explanation.* London: Oxford Univ. Press, 1957.
Mandelbaum, M. "Historical Explanation: The Problem of 'Covering Laws'," *History and Theory*, I (1961).
Passmore, J. "Explanation in Everyday Life, in Science, and in History," *History and Theory*, II (1962).
[See also essays in the section "Explanation and Laws" in *Theories of History*, P. Gardiner (ed.) Glencoe, Ill.: The Free Press, 1959.]